The Drive to Glory

The Drive to Glory

Behind the scenes with harness driver Ray Smith

By
Lynne M. Caulkett

E-BookTime, LLC
Montgomery, Alabama

The Drive to Glory
Behind the scenes with harness driver Ray Smith

This book is true and factual. Places, dates and events are based on word of mouth information, taped and phone conversations provided by Mr. Ray Smith and family. All information is deemed to be correct by the author, although minor inconsistencies may occur due to the number of years that have passed.

ISBN: 978-1-60862-268-9

First Edition
Published March 2011
E-BookTime, LLC
6598 Pumpkin Road
Montgomery, AL 36108
www.e-booktime.com

Printed in the United States of America
This book is printed on acid-free paper

Cover photo: Illustration provided by Harness Tracks of America, Inc.

About the Author photo (back cover): Photograph taken by Michael J. Currier

Other Books by Lynne M. Caulkett

Second Chances, Amazing Horse Rescues
Available at: www.uPUBLISH.com

Sweet Dreams
Available at: www.AuthorHouse.com

Blazing Glory
Available at: www.AuthorHouse.com

Silhouette's Black Diamond
Available at: www.E-BookTime.com

Big Smiles, Small Miracles
Available at: www.E-BookTime.com

Requiem of Innocence, Fortitude of a Champion
Available at: www.E-BookTime.com

So You Bought a Horse… Practical Guide to Horse Training
Available at: www.E-BookTime.com

Strike of the Hammer, A Guide to Understanding Your Farrier
Available at: www.E-BookTime.com

In Loving Memory of

Jim Caulkett
1943 – 2008

My heart, my soul, my love

Dedication

Bud and Pam Bertouille

Your constant support and friendship
is unending and far-reaching.
You both hold a special place in my heart
and in the hearts
of my children.

A special thanks to Ray and Marilyn

The lengthy conversations we had and the
wealth of information you both possess
made this book possible.

Acknowledgements

Ray and Marilyn Smith

Rejean Savard

Wikipedia

Harness Tracks of America

The Canadian Horse Racing Hall of Fame
Louis Cauz

Permission to use article, "Stanley Dancer As I Recall Him" granted in writing by writer, Dean Hoffman.

Permission to use "Illustration of a Harness" granted in writing by Pearson Scott Foresman.

Hoof Beats Publishing Supervisor, Nicole Kraft

Hoof Beats Publishing Assistant, Jason Turner

Editing help provided by Mary Ann Phyllis Spellman

Preface

The life of a jockey is as dangerous as it is exhilarating, and yet young men and women have been drawn to it for decades. Why? That was the answer I was searching for as I set out to write this book. While we have all heard of famous jockeys, such as Eddie Arcaro, Willie Shoemaker, Ron Turcotte, and Canadian-born harness driver Hervé Fillion, to name a few, what about the jockey's who don't make it big but follow the circuit day after day, year after year, to make a living around horses? What drives them to stay with it? In some cases they give up family, friends and a "normal" life, choosing instead to chase the dream of one day being on the back of that one special horse who will take them to the winner's circle. To understand the world of jockeys we first must understand what a jockey is.

In sport, a jockey is described as one who rides horses in horse racing or steeplechase racing, primarily as a profession. Jockeys are normally self-employed, nominated by horse trainers to ride their horses in races for a fee (which is paid regardless of the prize money the horse earns for a race) and a cut of the purse winnings.

Jockeys usually start out when they are young, exercising horses in the morning for the trainers, later entering the profession as apprentices. An apprentice jockey is known as a "bug boy", because the asterisk that follows their name in the program looks like a bug. All jockeys must be licensed and are not allowed to have an interest in a bet placed in a race. An apprentice jockey has a master, who is a horse trainer. After a period of time, the jockey becomes a senior jockey, developing a relationship with trainers and individual horses. Sometimes a senior jockey is paid a retainer by an owner, which gives the owner the right to insist that the jockey ride his or her horses in races.

The colors worn by jockeys in races are registered colors of the owner or trainers who employ them. The practice of horsemen wearing colors probably stems from medieval times when jousts were held between the knights. But racing held in Italian city communities since medieval times may have influenced the origins of racing colors of multifarious patterns that are seen today. Such traditional events are still held on town streets and are remarkable for the furious riding and the colorful spectacle they offer.

Getting breeches and bibs, stocks or cravats known as "silks" is a rite of passage when a jockey is first able to don silken pants and colors in their first race ride. At one time silks were invariably made of silk, though now synthetics are sometimes used instead. Nevertheless, the silks and their colors are important symbols evoking emotions of loyalty and festivity.

Jockeys have a reputation for being short, but there are no height restrictions. In thoroughbred racing a rider can be of any height if he/she can make weight but it is still generally limited to fairly short individuals because of the limits on a person's body. Jockey's typically range from 5' to 5'5 in height. While weight is not regulated in harness racing, it is advantageous for a rider to be lighter for obvious reasons. The less the horse has to pull, the quicker he will be.

Jockey's come from a wide range of ethnic and family backgrounds. Some carry on the family name as their fathers and grandfathers were trainers, horse owners, or jockeys themselves. Others seek the thrill of the profession or simply love to be around horses and have a passion for the sport of racing.

Possibly the most famous jockey of all times is Jorge Chavez. Born is 1961 in the poverty-stricken city of Callao, Peru, young Chavez worked for food and money. He began his horseracing career in 1982 in his native Peru and by 1987 was his country's leading rider. In April of 1988 he immigrated to the United States where he attained a great deal of success at Florida racetracks. Moving to New York a few years later, Chavez was the leading rider on the NYRA circuit from 1994 to 1999. During that time he rose to national prominence. He won two of the 1999 Breeders' Cup races, taking both the Distaff and the Sprint. During that year, Chavez also won the Cigar Mile Handicap for the second time in his career. As a result of his stellar year, Chavez also won the 1999 Eclipse Award for Outstanding Jockey.

A fan favorite on the New York circuit where Chavez rode for many years, he was affectionately known as "Chop Chop" by fans due to his distinctive riding style. His style of using the whip appeared to be relentless. However, this was more of a byproduct of having short arms due to his height of 4'10", as opposed to him being overly aggressive.

In 2000 he was voted the Mike Venezia Memorial Award for "extraordinary sportsmanship and citizenship". In 2001 Chavez rode Monarchos to victory in the Florida Derby, and then in America's most prestigious race, the Kentucky Derby. The following year he won the Woodward Stakes, however his career started to slow after suffering a broken back in a spill in the running of the 2003 Florida Derby race.

As of mid-summer 2006, Chavez was riding on the competitive Southern California circuit, which includes the Santa Anita Park, and the Del Mar Race Track. In 2007 Chavez returned to New York to compete at the Saratoga Race Course for the summer meet. After this meet, he returned to Belmont to ride. He has since been riding in Florida. His major racing wins number twenty-two, along with three American Classics/Breeders' Cup wins and two racing awards. The significant horses he rode over the years were Monarchos, Lido Palace, Behrens, and Albert the Great.

And who can forget the legendary Seabiscuit and his famous rider, Red Pollard. Trainer Tom Smith paired the horse with the Canadian jockey, who had experienced racing in the west and in Mexico, but was down on his luck. In 1936, the team raced for the first time in Detroit without impressing anyone. But improvements came quickly for Seabiscuit, and after several wins, including Detroit's Governor's Handicap, the horse was shipped by rail car to California. In his first race, the Bay Bridge Handicap, Seabiscuit started out badly, but ran through the fields before easing up to win the race by five lengths, in a time only three-fifths of a second off the world record.

In 1937 Seabiscuit won eleven of his fifteen races and was the leading money winner in the United States that year. He was now a celebrity and fans crowded the stands to catch a glimpse of this victorious horse. After a devastating injury during a training ride, Pollard lost sight in one eye, a fact that he hid during his career.

In 1938, as a five-year-old, Seabiscuit continued his success. Unfortunately, during that same year, Pollard suffered a terrible fall while racing on another horse, Fair Knightness. With Pollards chest crushed by the weight of the fallen horse, and his ribs and arm broken, the jockey began a painful and slow rehabilitation process.

Probably the greatest race remembered was Seabiscuit's match against the great three-year-old Triple Crown winner,

War Admiral. Still not able to ride, Pollard was replaced by George Woolf, a great rider and old friend of Pollard. November 1, 1938 was dubbed the "March of the Century", and the event itself, run over 1 and 3/16th miles was one of the most anticipated sporting events in U.S. history. The Pimlico Race Course in Baltimore, Maryland, was jammed solid with spectators from the grandstands to the infield. Trains brought in fans from all over the country with an estimated 40 million fans listening on the radio. War Admiral was the prohibitive favorite and a near unanimous selection of the writers and tipsters, excluding the California faithful.

Head-to-head races favor the fast starters, and War Admiral's speed from the gate was the stuff legends are made of. Seabiscuit, however was a pace stalker, skilled at holding with the pack before destroying the field with late acceleration. From the scheduled walk-up start, few gave him a chance to lead War Admiral into the first turn. However, Seabiscuit's rider, Smith, knew this and had been secretly training with the horse under the direction of Red Pollard using a starting bell and a whip to give the horse a burst of speed from the start.

When the bell rang, Seabiscuit ran away from the Triple Crown Champion. Despite being drawn on the outside,

Woolf led by a length after just twenty seconds. Halfway down the backstretch, WarAdmiral started to cut into the lead, gradually pulling level with Seabiscuit, and then slightly ahead. Following the advice he had been receiving from Pollard, Woolf had eased up on Seabiscuit, allowing him to see his rival and then asked for more speed. Two hundred yards from the wire, Seabiscuit lunged forward and continued to extend his lead over the closing stretch, finally winning by four clear lengths.

As a result of that overwhelming victory, Seabiscuit was named "Horse of the Year" for 1938.

And I don't think there is a horse lover in the world who didn't feel the profound grief of jockey Edgar Prado, one of the top jockey's, when in the spring of 2006 he rode Barbaro to a 6 ½ length victory at the Kentucky Derby, only to have the horse suffer a catastrophic leg injury two weeks later at the Preakness Stakes. After a noble effort to save the horse's life, Barbaro was finally put down, ending what could have been one of the most successful horses in history.

These examples are the stories we see and witness in the world of thoroughbred horse racing. But what does the life of a harness jockey, or “driver” as they are called, entail? What are the struggles that these men and women face and what do they sacrifice for the career they have chosen? In the pages ahead you will meet retired driver Ray Smith. The story that he tells exemplifies a real-life vision of what goes on behind the scenes, away from the Triple Crown races and the high profile horses. It is the story of a simple man who has a deep love for horses, an obsession for racing and the woman responsible for his career.

Chapter 1

Raymond Frellsen Smith was born on July 31, 1939, in Baskin, Louisiana to Percy and Marguerite Smith. When Ray was a mere two weeks old, his mother, the youngest of 13, saddled up her horse and rode, babe in arms to her mother's home ten miles away, so that Ray's grandmother could see the newborn for the first time. The Smith's lived in the swamps and had no car back then. People relied on their horses for transportation. By age two the boy was riding regularly, strapped to the saddle of a horse Ray's dad bought for a sack of flour and five dollars. That was Ray's first horse. Horses became a part of his daily life.

Life was hard on the family when Ray was young. The family was in deep debt, with no credit or savings, and in 1949, Ray's dad Percy got an offer to work on the pipeline. They offered him $500 a week clear. That was unheard of back then. It was big money and he couldn't turn it down. Percy accepted the job and took the family with him. But every three months they had to move to keep up with the pipeline. He would move the family 35 miles or so ahead of the pipeline, and when the work caught up to them, he would move again.

This meant that from the fifth to the eleventh grade, Ray went to 18 different schools! Ray describes himself as an 80 lb. weakling, skinny as a rail, and he suffered severe taunting from the students at each new school he attended. Being the new kid at school, he endured many beatings at the hands of the school bully's. As a result he became very confrontational, and when approached by anyone threatening him, he would retaliate with baseball bats, fists, or anything he could get his hands on to protect himself. He was tired of the beatings and a bad temper replaced his shyness. He had been beat up and called names enough times, and learned how to fight back.

But it took its toll on the young man. That bad temper followed him into his adult life. He had learned to fight and if anyone crossed him, that person got an "ass beating" as Ray describes. It wasn't until he was well into his 40's that he finally learned how to control his temper and became a gentler man. He credits his wife's patience, and karate classes for his change in character. The man he became is the man you will meet in the following chapters.

I met Ray in the spring of 2008 while having my kitchen remodeled. A handyman by trade, Ray accompanied the man who installed the new countertops, to complete any electrical work that needed to be done. At some point during the day, our conversation turned to horses. I mentioned that I was an equestrian writer, and Ray began telling me about some of his experiences as a harness driver. At the time I was considering ideas for a new book and my interest was immediately sparked. As Ray talked I knew immediately that I had found what I was looking for. Ray would become the topic of my new book.

A few months later, as I made plans to begin interviewing Ray for the book, I realized that I didn't know much about the sport. I was familiar with thoroughbred racing but not harness. So I began to research. Harness racing is a form of horse racing in which the horses race in a specified gait. They usually pull two-wheeled carts called sulkies.

In most jurisdictions harness races are restricted to Standardbred horses. Standardbreds are so named because in the early years of the Standardbred studbook, only horses that could trot or pace a mile in a "standard" time were entered into the book. The standard time was 2 minutes 30 seconds. Standardbreds have proportionally shorter legs than Thoroughbreds and longer bodies. They also have more placid dispositions, which suits horses whose races involve more strategy and more re-acceleration than do the Thoroughbred races.

Races can be conducted in two differing gaits: trotting and pacing. The difference is that a trotter moves its legs forward in diagonal pairs, right front and left behind, then left front and right hind striking the ground simultaneously, whereas a pacer moves its legs laterally, right front and right hind together, then left front and left hind.

Pacing races constitute 80% to 90% of the harness races conducted in North America. Pacing horses are faster and, more importantly, less likely to break stride (a horse that starts to gallop rather than pacing must be slowed down and taken to the outside until it regains stride, thus losing precious minutes during a race). One of the reasons pacers are less likely to break stride is that they often wear hobbles which are straps that connect the legs on each of the horse's sides. The belief that hobbles are used to create this gait is a misconception; the pace is a natural gait, the hobbles merely an accessory to support the pace at top speed.

Most harness races start from behind a motorized starting gate. The horses line up behind a hinged gate mounted on a motor vehicle, which then takes them to the starting line. At the starting line the wings of the gate are folded up and the vehicle accelerates away from the horses.

The sulky (informally known as a bike) is a light two-wheeled cart equipped with bicycle wheels. The driver (not called a jockey as in thoroughbred racing) carries a long, light whip, which is chiefly used to signal the horse by tapping and to make noise by striking the sulky shaft. There are strict rules as to how much the whip may be used.

Almost all North American races are at a distance of one mile and North American harness horses are all assigned a "mark" which is their fastest winning time at that distance. Harness races involve considerable strategy. Track size plays an important part here. On the smaller half-mile and five-eighths rings common to harness racing, early speed becomes a more important factor, while the longer stretch of seven eighths and one mile tracks lend themselves more favorably to closing efforts. Usually several drivers will contend for the lead out of the gate. They then try to avoid getting boxed in as the horses form into two lines, one on the rail and the other outside, in the second quarter mile. They may decide to go to the front, to race on the front on the outside ("first over", a difficult position), or to race with cover on the outside. On the rail behind the leader is a choice spot, known as the pocket, and a horse in that position is said to have a "garden trip". Third on the rail is an undesirable spot, known on small tracts as the "death hole".

As the race nears the three-quarter-mile mark, the drivers implement their tactics for advancing their positions, going to the lead early, circling the field, moving up an open rail, advancing behind a horse expected to tire, and so on. Unlike Thoroughbreds, harness horses accelerate during the final quarter mile of a race. The finishes of harness races are often spectacular and perhaps more often extremely close. The judges often have to request prints of win, place and show photos to determine the order of finish.

As in thoroughbred racing, harness racing also has its major derby races. The Trotting Triple Crown is made up of the Yonkers Trot, the Hambletonian, and the Kentucky

Futurity. The Hambletonian is sometimes referred to as the "Kentucky Derby of Harness Racing." The Triple Crown of Harness Racing for Pacers includes Cane Pace, held in Freehold, New Jersey, The Little Brown Jug, in Delaware, Ohio and the Messenger Stakes, in Yonkers, New York.

One other difference between Thoroughbred racing and harness racing is the acquisition of colors. As I mentioned earlier, jockeys who race Thoroughbreds wear the colors of the owners of the horse. In harness racing, the drivers each have their own colors, which they design and register with the Harness Racing Association. They wear these same colors no matter what horse they drive or who owns the horse. The cost of one silk outfit is about $400.00. Drivers need several different silks depending on weather, and use. For instance they usually have a short-sleeved outfit as well as a long-sleeved, and a rain outfit. Jumpsuits are also used for training. Some of the early drivers only used two colors while today they use up to four colors.

An example of a color combination can be illustrated in the outfit that Ray Smith designed for himself. He chose white for the body, yoke, sleeves and pockets, with the belt, collar and cuffs trimmed in turquoise. He had a turquoise "S" (for Smith) embroidered in the center front and back of his silk shirts and one turquoise star on each sleeve. Later he changed the turquoise to a dark blue.

I sat with Ray and his wife Marilyn in their kitchen one particular evening, and asked Ray how he got into racing. Here is Ray's story in his own words:

First of all let me explain how I met my wife, Marilyn. I was about 17 and had a white Lincoln with red interior. It was a sweet car. Back in those days, it was not uncommon for kids to race their cars. We knew some roads where the police didn't really patrol too often so it was a pretty fair bet that at certain times there would be races going on.

Well, one day my friend and I were driving and a couple of girls pulled up along side of us in a Crown Victoria. They challenged us to a race and we accepted. We figured we would have no problem beating them. But that was not the case. When we took off from a standstill, the girls stayed neck and neck with us. We finally agreed that it was an even match.

My friend suggested that we follow the girls to their house and that is exactly what we did. Now I really liked Eleanor and would have asked her out but it turned out she already had a boyfriend. Her other sister was married and that left Marilyn. Once I got to know her, I decided to ask her out. Now remember, I was only 17, but Marilyn was 21. When I asked her out, she turned me down flat. She said she would never date me; I was too young. Well, I kept at her and I finally told her that she had no choice. Once I graduated, I would join the Air Force and we would be married. She disagreed, but my mind was made up. That was pretty presumptuous of me wasn't it? (laugh)

Well, that turned out to be just what happened. I graduated, joined the service, we were married and she left for basic training with me. And we have been together ever since!

I got into horse racing because of my wife, believe it or not. I really never wanted to be a race driver. I had a good business and was making big money. I repaired heavy equipment and didn't want or need the money from horse racing. Anyway, Marilyn and I were driving down the road one day and we passed these people racing ponies on a track. Well, as I drove by my wife said, "Let's go back and see what they're doing. I want to see."

Well, you know what that's like. (laugh) When the wife asks you to do something, you'd better listen! I turned the car around and we went back and I ended up buying her a pony that day. From there we bought a sulky, a harness and she began driving. I thought to myself, "I don't want to drive no damn pony! I mean a pony is a pony." I figured that was a girl thing.

Marilyn absolutely loved it and before I knew it we had another pony. And I started to think, "Wait a minute, this looks like fun!" So I called up the guy that invented M&M candy, John McNamara, who dealt with ponies, and I bought Charlau's Madonna Racey from him for $3500.00 cash. Back in the 60's that was a lot of money. And, this horse was broke down! Her feet had quarter cracks, everything, and I still paid John $3500.00 for this pony.

We took her to Pennsylvania, fixed her up, put special shoes on her and I took her to the Meadows in that state, where we broke the World record! I was now in the racing business. What Marilyn started, I quickly became a part of and I loved it. We kept registering in more races with this pony and kept breaking records. (More about her in a later chapter) And then we bought R.M. Lee Volo, and he was the fastest stud we had seen. After that, we bought My Devotion, but I couldn't drive her. She didn't take too kindly to men so Marilyn took over driving her. I was driving fourteen pony races a day at the time and that is more than one person can handle so I didn't care that Marilyn drove My Devotion.

Well, she ended up beating me with that little mare! I was driving the fastest stud and she beats me. Of course I was hopping mad about that. I have never been a very good loser. But Marilyn was happy as can be! (laugh). I don't like to get beat, especially by my wife. She went on to embarrass me many times. But that is how the sport goes sometimes.

Later we ended up with the world's fastest pacing mare, fastest trotting mare, and a hackney, some Paso Fina's; oh my God we had everything. When we would go to big affairs and begin unloading our truck, in New York or Pennsylvania for instance, there would be fifty people, waiting there just to see these ponies! Can you imagine out of eight World champions, seven of them are going to walk off that truck? And they all belonged to us! It was quite a sight. The USTPA can verify our records. We were invited to go everywhere with these ponies.

Picture this: I would work all day, and when I got home on Friday, Marilyn would have the horses all loaded, all the carts up on top. All I had to do was to jump in the truck and start driving, and we would drive all night long sometimes to get from New Jersey to Ohio. We would go to Dayton and to Toledo and then drive all the way back on Sunday night after racing for two full days. And then I'd go to work and work all day Monday and come home Monday night and sleep. It was a harsh schedule. But we did it.

In time, it was Marilyn who bought our first full-size horse. She found this horse she wanted to buy for $5600.00. A friend owned a Standardbred that was for sale. She had decided that if she was going to race for money, she may as well race for big money! So she talked to me and said she wanted the horse and she needed $5600.00. I refused to give her the money. I told her I couldn't afford to take the time off of work because we were really busy and I wouldn't have the time for a horse. All of my spare time away from work was being taken up with the ponies. But that didn't stop Marilyn.

Determined, she took her new Ford Thunderbird to the bank (we had paid cash for it) and got a loan herself, using the car for collateral. That was at a time when you could shake someone's hand and make a deal with a banker. Marilyn bought the horse and that gelding, named Jay Ess Magic ended up making her $56,000.00 in New York!

Well, Marilyn gives the horse to this guy to train and the horse made her so much money it wasn't even funny. When we claimed him at first he was a $4000.00 claimer and later we took him to New York as a $27,000.00 claimer! Now I don't know if you understand what a claiming race is so I will explain it to you.

Say for instance, your horse is entered in a claiming race and you claim what the horse is worth, say $4000.00 like Jay Ess Magic was at first. So the horse is put within a group of horses that may not be conditioned like the big money horses. Before the race if a person wants to claim a certain horse, he has to put the money for the horse in a box and at then end of the race if that person's name is called, he now has paid for the horse and owns that horse. You retain the purse money for the race but you no longer own that horse.

So we were heartbroken when someone won Jay. I figured we had his claim high enough that no one would want him. But they did. And it was one of the biggest trainers in New York. Well, later that night, they start to walk the horse out of the wash area, and he was dead lame! And he had NEVER been lame before. We think he knew he was going with someone else and he broke down. These people who bought him couldn't believe it.

They took him to New York and started him out, let him rest, and once they began racing him they couldn't win anything! He lost race after race. Then they made a huge mistake. They put him in a claiming race for $10,000.00. I said to Marilyn, "Now we are getting him back!" I had $10,000.00 wadded up in my pocket, all in $100 dollar bills. I walked right up to the secretary, and put my money in the box and told her I was claiming Jay Ess Magic! They gave me a receipt and I was waiting at the receiving line after the race. The owners were laughing when I got him.

"You taking this piece of garbage?" they said, chuckling.

"Yep, I am," I replied as I walked him away.

We took that horse back to Freehold and worked with him for about a week and then I put him in a claiming race at $17,500.00. I knew no one would claim him. No one thought he was worth a thing. And we win! So now the next race I put him in at $20,000.00 and we win. Now we go back to New York and I put him in at $27,000.00 and we win. At this point they started writing Jay Ess Magic up in the newspapers. No one could figure out what happened. The top trainers couldn't do a thing with this horse and then the original owners, who have much less training background, take him back and no one can beat him! Believe me, we got a lot of publicity with that horse. From that time on no one would claim a horse from me.

Now that I was into racing with both feet, I got a taste of what it was like not only to be a driver but an owner and a winner as well. The daily care of the horses comes along with the package, though, at least for most people. I have to go a little off track here and tell you something about how I feel about grooming and doing the every day work with my horses. I am not a person who likes to clean up after the horses. That is what I pay a groom to do. But my trainer was from the old school and believed that if you're a driver then you have to muck stalls, throw hay and take a brush to your horse. It didn't matter to him if you were an owner or not. Well, that just wasn't my thing and I told him so. I figured that if I put up the money, and I'm the one sitting behind him on the track, why should I have to clean up after the horse? It made sense to me. But with much insistence, he put me to work one day.

"Okay, I'll clean that stall," I said, knowing full well that I would show him a thing or two.

Back then, they bedded the horses down with expensive straw, so the groomer would have to take the good straw and rake it into the corner, remove the manure and lay the saved stuff back down along with some fresh straw. You wanted to keep as much of the old stuff as you could to save money.

Well, I went in and took everything out! The trainer came back and when he saw what I had done he threw his hands up.

"What in the world are you doing?" he hollered.

"You told me to clean the stall, and now it's clean as hell," I replied calmly.

"You don't have to clean no more stalls," he quickly answered, as he walked away, shaking his head in defeat.

Then there was one other time when he asked me brush the horse and I asked him which end of the brush I should use. I made my point and he never asked me to do another thing after that. (laugh)

Back to the story, we were very successful with horses that no one else wanted. For instance, we went to the Meadowland sale one time, and they just finished a big race called the World Cup, and they had horses from Australia, Canada, France, Germany, Norway, Denmark, the United States, all over the world. They would race three races and then the winners would be determined. And afterward they would have a sale.

Well, there was a horse in there from New Zealand. His name was Allen Bell. They brought him in the ring and I swear to God he was huge, over 16 hands. And he was a mess. He had foundered, his ankles were swollen beyond belief, he could hardly move, and Marilyn starts bidding on him! I was flabbergasted! What in the world was this woman doing?

Marilyn told me that was the horse she wanted. She knew she could get him back to good health and race him. She just had that gut feeling and wanted to give him a chance. I tried to talk her out of it and told her we would buy a decent horse instead, any one she wanted. At the time we could afford to buy a good, sound horse. Besides, this guy was so big she'd have to get on a five-gallon bucket to even get on the horse! But she insisted and held her ground.

Now when I say that this horse was broken, I mean it! He was 12 years old. Unfortunately they broke him down so badly, that he couldn't race anymore. His one ankle would not even flex anymore. The other foot was dished and he had foundered. He also had an extremely bowed tendon. He had been the New Zealand champion. They had brought him to the United States because he was the best in New Zealand and he was entered in the World Cup. He won his leg and he actually went in 1:54 flat, which was fantastic since he was against the best horses in the world. The World Cup was a premier race where you had to be invited to race.

But now Allen Bell was at best a horse that needed to be put out to pasture. I could not believe that my wife actually wanted to bid on this horse. She turned out to be the only bidder. We got him for $1800. Wasted money if you asked me at the time. I made no bones about that.

We had a dirt ramp going into my truck, and it took 5-6 of us to walk him up into the truck. He could hardly move. So now he is on the truck and on the way home I am thinking, "How the hell are we going to get this worthless horse out of the truck?" So I pulled into a ditch where we could elevate my ramp and with two of us on each side, we finally got him down and into the barn. It was no easy task.

I was very unhappy about this situation, but Marilyn started working on him right away.

"We just don't need any horses like this, Marilyn," I said. "He's taking up a stall, feed, and basically we bought an $1800 piece of nothing!"

"He's my horse," she shot back, still working on Allen Bell.

"Well, it's your money too!"

In a short amount of time I hate to admit it, but I had to eat those words. In two weeks time, the horse was walking. In a month's time, the ankle was flexing and the horse was much sounder. In that time, we never jogged him or put a harness on him. We only worked him in the pool. We swam that horse for about 2 minutes the first day and worked up to 45 minutes with a prod and whip behind him making him really work his muscles. After that we'd take him out of the water, rub him down and then back in.

What you have to remember is that he already was a world champion. He knew how to race, but needed to be built back up again so he COULD race! We didn't have to teach him anything. After a month or so Marilyn decided that it was time to start jogging him slowly. I didn't think he was ready, but she felt he needed to get back into the mindset of racing again.

So she put a harness on him, which was funny in itself. Here is this tiny woman standing on a 5-gallon bucket trying to harness this huge horse. But, she did it! Once Marilyn set her mind to something there was no talking her out of it!

(laugh) But we found out quickly that this wasn't any ordinary horse.

Turns out that this horse, although injured, was strong as all get-out. He could kick a 2x12 inch plank in the stall wall and break it just like a toothpick. We kept our bikes up above the stalls and when he broke the stall boards the bikes would go flying. He was one mean horse! He'd rear up on his hind legs with the race bike on and walk on his hind legs with you sitting in the cart! He was rough to drive. I thought to myself, "Man what have we done?"

I guess I should have never doubted Marilyn though, when she wanted to buy this horse. What no one else knew was that Marilyn was acquainted with a little old Amish man named Moe Schepler and while everyone thought he was a little on the odd side because he didn't talk to people much, he was a good horseman, probably one of the best around. Moe had his own remedies and he took a liking to Marilyn. He'd mind his own business, but when Marilyn bought Allen Bell, it was Moe's remedies that got the horse back on his feet.

Prior to that, in fact quite a long time before Marilyn bought Allen Bell, we bought a horse by the name of Jetlite.

Jet also had injuries, but Moe was convinced along with Marilyn that he could repair the damage Jet had suffered. I had Jet at Brandywine one night and I pulled him three wide and I shouldn't have and when I reached up and popped him one he went full out. That was the kind of horse he was. Well, the track was not good that night. It had been dug it up pretty bad and Jet must have slipped and tore that tendon right out. Moe was watching the race, and beat us back to the barn. When we got there he went right up to Marilyn. She had a reputation for being the best groom around and he knew it.

"Ma'am, you don't know me but I can fix that horse. I love that horse, he's a great, great horse," Moe said, after examining Jet. He was familiar with this horse and was convinced that Jet could do great things if given a chance.

"Okay, what do I do?" Marilyn asked.

"I'm going to give you some white stuff and some red stuff in bottles. I want you to use it the way I tell you," he answered, not explaining what the ingredients were.

Now Moe normally didn't share this with anyone. And he wouldn't let anyone else but Marilyn have the remedy. He instructed her to first put the white liquid on, followed by the red and then to wrap the leg up tight and do this everyday without fail, and that the horse would come back fine.

I was skeptical I'll admit it. This horse was worth a lot of money and I didn't want to take the word of some Amish man who may not know what the heck he was doing. Marilyn could do what she wanted with the bottles Moe gave her, but I decided to first take the horse to the University of Pennsylvania in Brandywine, only about ten miles away, to be checked out. The head veterinarian just happened to be on duty that day. So we have the horse x-rayed and the vet doesn't like what he sees.

"I'm afraid this horse is in bad shape. We can cut him open and take a chip off the broken bone and maybe in a year or so you could jog him and possibly race him again, but I don't know," the vet said.

So Marilyn tells the doctor to go ahead with the surgery and do what he had to do and then to make her an appointment for thirty days from then. She wanted to work on Jetlite and then bring him back in a month for a sonogram to see if the Amish man's tonics worked.

The vet understood that Marilyn want to help this horse, but was insistent that in thirty days there would not be any change in this horse. He'd still have the scarring and the injury, and there was probably nothing more that the doctor could do for the horse.

Marilyn held her ground and the vet did the surgery that was suggested. After the surgery, we took Jet back to the barn and every day for the next month Marilyn worked on the horse using the red and white concoction Moe Schepler had given her. She followed his instructions to a tee. The strange thing about the tonics, were that despite the red color of the one, when the wraps were removed, there was no evidence of any color! I have no idea what was in that potion, but we were always amazed that the wraps would be clean as a whistle when removed! Regardless, in thirty days we went back for our appointment at the University clinic.

The technician there prepped Jetlite, applied the gel and began the sonogram. Now understand that the horse had walked into the clinic perfectly sound. As the tech began looking for the injury, nothing showed up! So now they checked the tattoo number, thinking it was a different horse. You couldn't mistake this horse! But they had to check. So they clipped the hair from the leg and did another sonogram. And nothing! Well, they got on the phone and called the head vet and told him that they couldn't find anything, not even a scar from where he had cut the horse a month ago!

"I'll be there in thirty minutes," the vet said. This vet had retired a week or so before, but wanted to be called when Jet was brought back in.

When the vet arrived, he told the assistant to set up the sonogram and he wanted to do it himself. The sonogram began and the vet was visibly puzzled. He asked for the chart on the horse and the paperwork of the surgery he did on the horse. He checked his notes, that told him what the injury was and which leg it was, thinking he maybe was viewing the wrong leg. But he wasn't. It was the correct leg. The horse was sound and there was no indication of any injury!

The vet turned around and said, "I've been a vet here for more than thirty years, in fact I just retired. I've known this horse and he is a terrific horse, but I also know the injury he had. It was a devastating injury. Marilyn, I don't know what the hell you did, and I really don't want to know what you did, but when one of my good race horses breaks down, he's coming to you!"

As a vet, that doctor had never seen anything like this.

"Doc, I just fixed him," Marilyn said matter of factly.

So the next week we started jogging the horse, trained him and that horse went ahead and raced for four more years, broke track records and he was one of our best horses. And this was the horse no one wanted! He raced against the best horses in the world. In a short time he was considered invitational (tracks invited him to come and race and made sure we had anything we wanted when we arrived), and Jetlite was an outstanding animal.

I remember one time I raced Jetlite (more about him in the next chapter), against a fellow who had driven Jet for us in the stake races. His name was Mickey McNichol and he had the fastest double-gaited horse in the world at Pompano at that time. The horse's name was Speedy Romeo. During the race the other driver had the rail and I had the three-hole and he wasn't going to let me get to the top because he knew if I did there would be no stopping me, and he wouldn't be able to get around me. The horse he had would make a break from the gate every once in a while and I decided we were going to have a little duel.

Now there were six horses in this race and they were the best in the country at that time. We left the starting gate and we hit the eighth pole in about 11.1 seconds. We get down to the quarter in about 27 seconds and we start digging a hole. I was driving with two fingers and I just sat back and let my horse cut the mile. He can't let anyone else go in front of him now. When we hit that eighth pole those other horses had to be sixty feet behind us! After the race that other driver said that in all of his years racing, he had never seen a horse get to that eighth pole that fast. Jetlite was racing so fast at that point that the hobbles had already got up under his chest. He wasn't even using those hobbles!

This horse was so exceptional that if you wanted to lead, you just touched him but if you didn't want him to lead you just didn't touch him. You could drive him any way you wanted. He didn't care. He was such a smart, gentle animal. He made us a lot of money. And one funny thing about this horse, every morning he had to have a glazed donut! He didn't want any other kind; it had to be glazed. Marilyn made sure Jet always had his morning donut! And the only apple he would eat was a Macintosh. You give him anything but that kind and he would turn his head. You don't think they have personalities? They sure do."

Back to Allen Bells, story, once we started jogging him, it wasn't long before he was in top shape again. It was time to qualify him. I always had the fear though that he would hurt someone. I didn't like anyone else driving him. He was so bad in the paddock that when we came out for the parade to the starting gate, he would come out rearing, with the hobbles on and everything. And you're sitting in the bike, flat on your back, looking up at him as he walked on his hind legs. I'll tell you, he could make you very leery sitting behind him. He'd scare the crap out of most drivers. But at that time in my life I had been through so much I didn't much care about anything. I didn't have any fear and didn't care how rough the horse was that I drove. I just did it.

Anyway, I had misgivings about qualifying Allen Bell. I thought it was too soon and didn't want to see him injured again. I mean, his ankle looked good and could flex, and the foundered foot was getting much better. When you have a foundered foot like that, the farrier puts on what you call a bar shoe, which has a piece that comes up and hits on the frog, and that is what starts to straighten the coffin bone up again. I put a lot of effort into putting the right kind of shoe on him. Think about it, no feet, no horse!

But Marilyn had confidence in Allen Bell, so I sent my son-in-law to Cherry Hill with him for qualifying. But I gave him strict instructions not to let the horse go full out. I wanted to qualify him at around 2 minutes, and no more. I was so afraid of hurting this horse and we had come so far with his recovery. So my son-in-law comes back and tells me that the horse qualified in 57 seconds! I was hopping mad. I wanted to pop him right in the nose.

"How could you be this stupid? You have a horse that was broke down, what do you want to do, break him again in a qualifier? We put all this money in the horse and you want that to go to waste?" I was really hot and he knew it.

My son-in-law was an ex-hockey player. There was no reason he couldn't have helped this horse and held him back to keep him from an injury, or so I thought.

"Ray, I swear to you I had a death grip on him the whole way. I could NOT hold him back any more than I was. I choked him down almost! I couldn't hold him."

"Bull shit," I said. "There isn't a horse you can't hold if you want to."

I figured what was done, was done, the horse didn't break down, so we would go on from there.

"Well, just forget about it then, but from now on, I drive this horse, and no one else!"

So now we enter a race, and they cancel it. We put him back in a race again and I'll be damned if one of my other horses, Number Won Sun doesn't get called to race the same night in New York. Now I am in a quandary. I have to drive the New York race. I am not about to let anyone else drive

Number Won Sun and me drive Allen Bell, when I knew Allen Bell wouldn't be anywhere near a win. I figured he would end up dead last anyway. And the race in New York was a $30,000 race, which meant a $15.000 paycheck for me plus the bet. Where would you go?

So I sent my son and son-in-law with Allen Bell, and told them that whatever they did, don't let him get hurt! I didn't care where he finished. This was just a prep race and didn't matter. It was just training.

Well, later that night I called down to the track from New York and talked to one of the judges.

"You want the bad news or the good news first?"

"Gimme the bad news first. Did he kill someone?" I asked, cringing.

"No he didn't kill anyone," the judge laughed. "The bad news is that he didn't win."

"Well, I figured he wouldn't. What's the good news?"

"He missed winning by a half a nose in 1:54 flat."

I was stunned. I didn't know what to say.

So I get back to the farm late that night and of course, my kids were already back with Allen Bell.

"What happened?" I asked. "I told you to take it easy with the horse."

My son-in-law was the first one to speak.

"Ray, I sat dead last and never moved him up. We had less than a quarter of a mile to go and I reached up and tapped him. I figured we weren't going anywhere, and they wouldn't be able to say I wasn't trying. And then this damn horse almost jerked me back out of the cart. This horse could fly! He went from dead last on the outside and he went, woosh! Right up to the front."

Well, we had to get a tape of the race because I could not believe it. Everyone wanted to know what the hell we had done to this horse. He was a throw-away no one wanted, we got him dirt cheap for $1800 and I had no expectations. This was all Marilyn's doing.

I got lots of questions from people who thought we had shot him up with something, which we had not.

That horse came back as good as he was when he was in the World Cup. We even had him x-rayed and the calcium deposits around the ankles had all but worked their way out of the foot. He was as sound as he could be.

We raced Allen Bell until he was 14 years old. After that you can't race them anymore. We wanted a good retirement for him so we went to a farm in Maryland where they take horses that have finished their racing career and they turn them out on to 300 acres of grassy meadow to graze and relax. We could have sold him, but I thought he deserved to be turned out and have a good life. He was an amazing horse, that's for sure.

Chapter 2

Author's note: In 1977, Ray came across a three-year-old horse, co-owned by an English trainer, whose sire was Dancer Hanover. Dancer was a great horse named after Stanley Dancer. Stanley was an American harness racing driver and trainer. He was the only horseman to drive and train three Triple Crowns in horse racing history. In total, he drove 23 Triple Crown winners. He was the first trainer to campaign a horse, Cardigan Bay to $1 million in a career in 1968 and drove the Harness Horse of the Year seven times. During his career, he won over $28 million and was called by the United States Trotting Association, "perhaps the best-known personality in the sport."

Dancer was born in West Windsor Township, New Jersey on July 25, 1927, and grew up on a farm in New Egypt, New Jersey, living in this area for almost his entire life on a 160-acre farm with a half-mile training track before moving to Pompano Beach, Florida in 1999. He dropped out of school after the eighth grade.

He borrowed silks for his first race, driving a horse he had bought for $75 using money he had won from a 4-H club. He started driving horses at Freehold Raceway in 1945, winning his first race the following year. Dancer started his stable in 1948 with a trotter he had bought using $250 of his wife's college savings. That horse, Candor, took home $12,000 during the following three years.

A spindly 5-feet 8-inches, and weighing in at 135 pounds, Stanley was described by Red Smith, another driver, as not looking "old enough to be let out for night racing." Despite his size and youthful looks, he used an aggressive, all-out style right from the start, and retained his aggressive methods despite 32 racing spills (including a 1955 incident in which he broke his back), four car accidents, and crashes in both an airplane and a helicopter, as well as two heart attacks during his driving career. He had been given a physician's recommendation to quit racing, but declined to take the advice, noting that, "There is nothing dangerous about harness racing. The worse crack-up I had ever been in was an auto accident."

In a six-horse field at the 1961 International Trot at Roosevelt Raceway, Dancer drove Su Mac Lad finishing in a time of 2:34.4 in driving rain and a sloppy track in front of 28,105 racing fans, with the French horse, Kracovie in second by what the New York Times called "the smallest of noses" with American horse, Tie Silk in third. The victory made Su Mac Lad the first American horse to take the title.

Dancer drove New Zealand horse, Cardigan Bay to $1 million in winnings in 1968, the first harness horse to surpass that milestone. Dancer and Cardigan Bay even appeared together on the Ed Sullivan Show. In 1995, in his final race, he rode Lifelong Victory to a win in the New Jersey Sires Stakes held at Garden State Park in Cherry Hill, New Jersey.

He earned $1 million in purses in 1964, becoming the first driver to win that much in a single year, and drove Cardigan Bay, the first Standardbred horse to win $1 million in career prize money. He drove his 3781st and final winner in 1995, bringing in $28,002,426 during his career as a driver. He won the Triple Crown three times, with trotters Nevele Pride in 1968, and Super Bowl in 1972, and with pacer, Most Happy Fella in 1970. He trained/drove the harness horse of the year seven times, with trotters Su Mac

Lad in 1962 and Nevele Pride in 1967 through 1969 and with the pacers Albatross in 1971 and 1972 and Keystone Ore in 1976. He won the Hambletonian four times and was inducted into the Harness Racing Hall of Fame in 1969.

After surgery to treat an intestinal ailment, his beloved horse Dancer's Crown died three weeks before the 1983 Hambletonian, a horse that would have been favored to win the race. Dancer reluctantly entered the little-known, Duenna at the insistence of his family and friends, and won the race, the first filly to win the race in 17 years. Golfer, Arnold Palmer called the victory, "one of the most dramatic moments in sports!"

Dancer died at age 78 on September 9, 2005 in his home in Pompano Beach, Florida due to complications from prostate cancer.

The following is an article published by sports writer, Dean A. Hoffman shortly after Stanley Dancer's death. It epitomizes how the harness racing world felt about Mr. Dancer.

Stanley Dancer As I Recall Him

Thursday, September 8, 2005 - by Dean A. Hoffman

It's difficult to comprehend today how much Stanley Dancer dominated harness racing in his prime.

Maybe the names of some of his horses will help: Albatross. Nevele Pride. Most Happy Fella. Super Bowl. Keystone Ore. Henry T. Adios. Su Mac Lad. Cardigan Bay. Noble Victory. Bonefish. Duenna. Egyptian Candor. Lehigh Hanover.

The list goes on and on, just as Dancer's legacy will go on and on.

USTA Photo

Dancer was frequently honored at banquets for superstars in the world of sports and here he chats with the football legend Red Grange in the 1960s.

Dancer died today in Florida after enduring years of pain that left him a virtual invalid. He turned 78 on July 25 and poor health in recent years prevented him from being part of the sport that consumed his life as a younger man.

Stanley Dancer drove horses to win, and Stanley Dancer drove himself to win. He came off a New Jersey dairy farm to reach the absolute pinnacle of his profession. Whenever they list the greatest of harness racing's greats, you'll find the name Stanley Dancer.

He competed at the highest levels of the sport, and there was no one better at campaigning a horse in the sport's stratosphere. He won the Jug and Hambo four times. And he won it as both the trainer and the driver of the winner. (His first Hambo victory came as the trainer of Egyptian Candor in 1965 when he turned the reins over to his friend Del Cameron.)

From 1962-72, Dancer trained and drove the Horse of the Year six times.

He had the best owners. He bought the best yearlings. He ran a spit 'n' polish stable. And he attracted outrageous animosity and jealousy from lesser people. I'll never forget the shameful spectacle of Dancer and Albatross being booed during the 1971 Jug. People were simply resentful of his overwhelming success.

Invariably you'd hear horsemen in that era lament, "If I had the stock that Dancer gets to train, I'd have some champions, too."

But what they failed to mention is that no one gave Stanley Dancer all those high-priced yearlings with glittering pedigrees. He earned the confidence of wealthy owners with his abilities and his accomplishments and his dedication to his absolute excellence.

Stanley Dancer was not an educated man. He quit school to pursue his passion for horses. It was in the world of horses and racing that he found himself, and found his fame and fortune. When it came to harness racing, Stanley Dancer was, as Shakespeare wrote of Hamlet, "to the manner born." He found his calling and he used his gifts.

USTA Photo

It's another effortless win for Dancer and Nevele Pride. The surly-tempered trotter was Horse of the Year each season he raced and broke Greyhound's 31-year-old speed standard for trotters in 1969.

Dancer had a gift with horses, an innate ability to spot extraordinary horses and to get the most from them on the track. Many of his champions he broke and developed, but others—Su Mac Lad, Albatross, Keystone Ore, for example—he took over other trainers. They were "made" horses when Dancer got them, but he made them better.

Dancer revolutionized racing on the half-mile tracks at Yonkers and Roosevelt in the 1950s by bursting out of the gate, seizing control of the race, and daring anyone to challenge him. While waiting for the inevitable challenge, Dancer rested his horse and was thus able to rebuff his pursuers.

It was a tactic that worked even when Dancer's stock raced on the roomy mile tracks of the Grand Circuit. If there was one trait that marked a Dancer horse it was gate speed. His horses the manners of a diplomat behind the gate and the speed of a sprinter when the starter said "Go."

I had the good fortune to speak with Stanley many times about his horses and I've never encountered a horseman with better recall of details than he had. He could spell out the details of Noble Victory's shoeing and his propensity to hit his shins two decades after the horse retired. He remembered the fractions of miles that most people had long since forgotten.

He remembered such details because he was so intensely focused on his craft and was such a perfectionist.

His career is well known and will be documented in other stories. His name began to surface in racing summaries after World War II, and the kid from the dairy farm, like crème, rose to the top.

He won five races at Yonkers in 1951—four of them in a row. Long before the era of catch-drivers, such a feat was incomprehensible. Afterwards Dancer got a congratulatory telegram from Delvin Miller, and he was so proud that he carried that telegram in his wallet for years.

Dancer's rise to stardom paralleled the career of Billy Haughton and ironically Dancer got his name in the world record tables for the first time in 1955 when he catch-drove Belle Action to victory at Yonkers. He was just 28 years old.

In 1957 Hanover Shoe Farms honored Dancer by naming a superbly bred baby after him. A year later Dancer was at Harrisburg and had the final bid when Dancer Hanover sold for $105,000, the first Standardbred (or Thoroughbred) yearling to sell for six figures.

In 1961 Dancer won the Jug with Henry T. Adios and repeated the next year with Lehigh Hanover. That year he also campaigned the aged trotter Su Mac Lad to Horse of the Year honors.

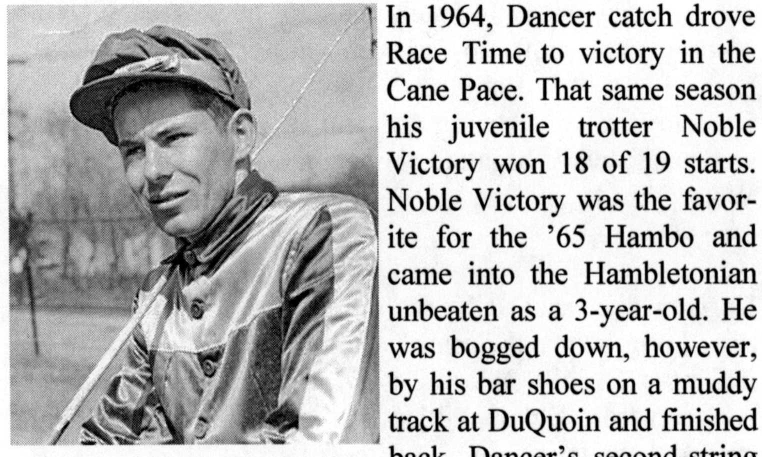

USTA Photo

In this photo from more than a half-century ago, Dancer was a young horseman making a meteoric rise in harness racing.

In 1964, Dancer catch drove Race Time to victory in the Cane Pace. That same season his juvenile trotter Noble Victory won 18 of 19 starts. Noble Victory was the favorite for the '65 Hambo and came into the Hambletonian unbeaten as a 3-year-old. He was bogged down, however, by his bar shoes on a muddy track at DuQuoin and finished back. Dancer's second-string colt Egyptian Candor took home the trophy in a four-heat epic.

In 1967 he brought out a trotting colt the likes of which the sport hadn't seen for years. His name was Nevele Pride and he would never win any congeniality awards, but he won 57 of his 67 career races. He gave Dancer his first Hambo win.

On Jan. 29, 1969, Dancer was the guest speaker at the annual banquet of the Indiana Trotting & Pacing Horse Assn. and he told the Hoosier horsemen that Nevele Pride would come to Indianapolis that summer and break Greyhound's 31-year-old world record of 1:55-1/4 by trotting in 1:54.3.

On Aug. 31, 1969, Nevele Pride took to the mile track at Indianapolis in pursuit of Greyhound's record and responded with a 1:54.4 mile that made him the fastest trotter in history.

In 1970, Dancer and Most Happy Fella swept the Triple Crown for pacers despite facing a relentless rival in Columbia George.

With Most Happy Fella retired in 1971, Dancer added the freshman champion Albatross to his stable and campaigned him to Horse of the Year honors and $558,009 in earnings, then a seasonal record.

Albatross won 25 of 28 races as a 3-year-old, and two of those losses were in the Little Brown Jug, a defeat that haunted Dancer for the remainder of his life.

Albatross was the best pacer in the sport again in 1972, and Dancer had the best trotter in the Triple Crown winner Super Bowl. This was Dancer's third Triple Crown horse in four years, but the final leg didn't come easy. Super Bowl's right sulky tire was punctured in both heats and only Dancer's masterful driving prevented an accident.

Bonefish won the Hambletonian in '75 and the next year Dancer had another Horse of the Year in Jug winner Keystone Ore.

In 1983, Dancer's career came full circle when he won the Hambletonian in his native state of New Jersey driving the filly Duenna.

Soon thereafter, he began to curtail the size of his stable drastically. He was increasingly bothered by back injuries he'd suffered during earlier in his career.

In the fall of 1993, Dancer took only a handful of yearlings into training and yet when the Meadowlands staged its summer classics for young trotters, Dancer's horses were ready. Donerail won the Peter Haughton Memorial and Lifelong Victory was second in the Merrie Annabelle. No, the old master hadn't lost his touch.

USTA Photo

Most Happy Fella sails to victory in the 1970 Messenger for Dancer before a packed house at Roosevelt Raceway on Long Island. Trailing him was his archrival Columbia George.

In 2003, Dancer was honored by Harness Tracks of America at the Nova Awards banquet in Florida. He came into the room on a walker and I was shocked at his frailty. His mind was sharp, however, and the attendees that night gave harness racing's lion in winter a warm and heartfelt reception.

Dancer's final years were not comfortable. Physical problems overwhelmed the drive and desire that had taken him to the top of the sport. The man who loved to talk about his horses and the sport grew reclusive as his energy waned.

His contributions to harness racing will never wane, however. He dominated the sport during its brightest years and champions that will never be forgotten.

Ray interjected this story about Stanley Dancer:

Before I tell you about how I acquired Jetlite, I have to tell you a little about Stanley Dancer. He helped me a lot. When I first started out with ponies, Stanley let me use all of his facilities. He was about as big time as they came. Before Stanley, drivers used to sit in the hole until the ¾ pole and they would try to make their move. That was the old kind of racing. We didn't wear helmets back then, only caps. And then here comes a guy named Stanley Dancer who was a hot shot, a potato farmer by trade. He had a trotter that was real good and he and his wife hauled that old trotter around until he made the big time. And believe me there wasn't anyone back then bigger than that man. All of his brothers and some nephews became drivers. He was a great person to know.

Stanley actually changed the way horse races were done. His idea was, "If I can make it to the front and I can keep on the front end, I can control the race. I can back up into your face, I can make you grab your horse or I can make you pull over and park it. Now you have to use your horse a lot harder out here than I have to use mine, just by sitting up here in front. So I have you beat to a point."

That was his philosophy and by God, it worked. When he started doing it, he won. He taught me that if you want to win, you have to dominate the race. That is how I ended up with seven World champion ponies out of eight. I took this information and applied it to my racing. I figured if I could get on the front end at the start of the race, the other drivers would have to come around me. I had a trotter that was so good no other trotter would race against him. They would make me race pacers, which were much faster than trotters and we still beat them. One of the best trotters I drove was R.M. Lee Volo.

If you watch drivers even today, you will see them using that same technique. And they have Stanley Dancer to thank for that.

Author's note: When Ray Smith first cast eyes on the three-year-old named Jetlite, he recognized the half-brother of Irish Kam, who had placed with a time of 1:57 on the race circuit, which was unheard of in those days. Jetlite's training was not going according to plan, however, even though with his lineage he was expected to become a highly sought after pacer.

Ray continues with his account of the story:

As a two-year-old and having a brother that was a spectacular racehorse, it was an accepted fact that Jetlite would follow in his footsteps. But being gangly and untrained, the owners could do nothing with this horse. He was growing very fast and he just didn't know how to race. So the owners decided to turn him out and bring him back the following year as a three-year-old. Well, in the meantime, my daughter, Debra had worked with this horse, so when he was brought back the following year, the owners should have given him to her to train. She had a great rapport with the horse and understood what he needed. The owners didn't see it that way, though and turned him over to a lazy trainer (my opinion) who took many short cuts and didn't intend to put the work in that Jetlite required.

The "training" that Jet was getting was no more than a quick gallop around the track in the morning followed by this guy throwing a blanket over the horse, returning him to the stable telling everyone he had "worked the heck out of the horse." And then the trainer would head to the racetrack to bet the horses. This horse was getting deprived of proper training, unbeknownst to the owners.

In the meantime, I had eight or nine horse I had taken to Saratoga for this trainer, and he asked me to go to the farm one day and help train Jetlite and another horse. He instructed me to check out the second horse, and if he was too crippled just to let him know and he would send him to the Amish. Well, I took him once around the track and put him right back in the barn. I wasn't going to brutalize a horse. This horse was extremely crippled. So after the horse was put away, I asked the trainer, who happened to be there at the time, to harness up Jetlite so I could take him out.

Now you have to understand that this trainer was extremely lazy. He balked when I asked him, but he reluctantly harnessed the horse up. When he put the equipment on Jet, he used a blind bridle, (bridle with blinders so the horse cannot see anything but straight ahead), no knee boots, no scalpers, and when I take the horse out, he acts like he doesn't know what to do! So I thought, "Whoa, wait a minute. A good lookin' horse like this that I know has the breeding and background should be able to perform." I knew that the owner was prepared to sell this horse and around the track the word was that he was asking $7500.00. He figured he would at least get that much out of this horse who didn't show much promise (according to the trainer).

So I said to the trainer, who was standing outside, not interested in hanging around, "Look, go ahead to the track. I'll work with this guy." Really I just wanted to get rid of the trainer, knowing how useless he was. Once he was gone, I went to the equipment room and picked out an open bridle (no blinders), a pair of knee boots, some scalpers (tendon boots), re-harnessed the horse, and I took him out a second time.

My way of training is to take the horse out on a float trip, then another trip around and finally a third. Now on the second time around, I bumped Jet a bit, and bam! That horse took off like a racehorse! He could see me, he didn't feel closed in and he relaxed and just ran. He wasn't hitting himself like he had without the knee boots and scalpers. So I brought him back in and cooled him down and then I took him out for the third round.

There wasn't anyone else around this farm that day but me. So I knew I could put a stopwatch on him. At that point I was interested in buying him so I wanted to see what he could do, but I didn't necessarily wanted anyone else to see. I turned him around using a jog cart, not a race bike, because this was a farm track not a racetrack. If you can go a quarter-mile in about 32 seconds you are doing good on this kind of a track. Well, I reached up and tapped him and he did a quarter in 30 seconds just like that! Now I am watching my watch and I don't believe what I am seeing. I said to myself, "Holy cow, what kind of a horse is this?"

I eased up on him and let him do the middle half of the course pretty easy. We get down to the last half, and I reached up and tapped him one more time to see what he would do and he kicked into another gear. It was amazing. I looked around to make sure no one was looking and slowed the horse down and we headed back to the barn. I put everything (the equipment) back just the way it was so no one would realize I had used it.

Once the horse was put away, I went home and told my wife I was going to buy this horse. She said I was nuts. She knew from my daughter, Debbie, that this horse had been so dumb that outside the barn was a big pile of manure and this horse would walk up atop the pile and lay down! I agreed that he did crazy things, but think about it. He was all cooped up, had blinder on, he couldn't see much of anything, so this damn horse didn't know what he was doing! He just needed someone to spend a little time with him.

That night I went to the owner's house. I noticed a big picture of the horse framed on the wall. Evidently he had bought the horse (with a partner) for his wife. They really thought he was going to be a great horse.

"I really want to buy this horse," I said to the owner.

"Well, I don't know," the man said hesitantly. "I was thinking about sending him to Freehold to be trained by you."

"Look," I said, a little irritated. "Is he for sale or not? If he is not for sale, don't tell all your friends at the farm that he is, and then have me train him and you sell him after all. And if he is not for sale, just let me know right now, one way or another. Do you want to sell him or not?"

"Well, I want to sell him but I have this partner, and I want $10,000.00," the man responded coyly. "I want $7500.00 now and I'll take $2500.00 in cash separate."

"I'll give you the money," I said, knowing now that the man intended to pocket the $2500.00 without telling his partner. But that was none of my concern. I just wanted that horse and I wasn't about to haggle. "I only brought $7500.00 with me, but as soon as I get my check cashed this week I'll bring the remaining money, but he is my horse now, right?"

"Oh yeah, we have a deal. The horse is yours," he quickly added. "I'll sign the papers right now."

"What about your partner? Doesn't he have to sign too?"

"Now don't you say anything to my partner about our deal, understood?"

"That's none of my business. I'm not saying anything," I said. "I just want to be sure the horse is mine. Where is your partner now?"

"He's in Delaware racing in the Stakes, and he won't be back for a week. But, don't worry he'll sign the papers," he assured me.

The deal was done, except for the final signature, but I took possession of the horse.

So I take the horse to Freehold the next week, and I got a pretty good trainer, an old guy who's real smart with horses. I told him what I had done out there at the farm and asked him not to say anything to anyone. I figured we would re-rig the horse, change the hobbles, put some boots on him and change his shoes. I had done some shoeing and knew how I wanted his feet to be done.

I did all of that and at the time we had a pretty good old horse in the barn that had won us a lot of money, called Barron Wally. We got him real cheap and took him all the way up to claim $20,000.00. He was a nice little horse. So I told the old trainer that I wanted to train Jetlite against Barron Wally.

"I know I can't beat Barron, but it will give me some indication of what Jet can do against a good horse," I explained

"I don't think Jet is in the same class with Barron," the trained said, shaking his head.

"That's okay, I bought him anyway, and we'll just see."

We took both horses out on the track and I sat in behind Jet in the first half-mile, and then I decided that now I would find out if he had any horse in him. I took him out of the hole and he went past Barron like he was sitting still.

"I don't believe what I just saw," said the flabbergasted trainer. "What kind of a horse is that?"

"I don't know," was all I could reply. This horse was still surprising me. "But he looks like a hell of a horse to me. He's got so much power. I've never let him go a whole mile. He doesn't have enough experience yet because he hasn't been properly trained. He needs his stamina built up. But we got something here for sure."

The trainer nodded his head in agreement. This horse was amazing indeed.

We kept Jet at the barn for about a week or a week and a half and jogged him every day and fed him real good. I told my son, Scott, that I wanted him to qualify this horse, because I couldn't do it.

"If I qualify him and they see me on this horse, they are going to wonder what is going on," I explained. "And you need to ride more to get your license so this will benefit both of us. Now here is what I want you to do. Just go qualifying time, don't go crazy with him. We just want to be within 2-3 seconds of the lowest qualifying time, understand?"

"Yes," he answered in agreement. "All I'm going to do is qualify."

So Scott came back to me later in the day, and he was pretty excited.

"Boy, that's a nice horse," he exclaimed.

"I know, but don't you go saying anything to anyone yet."

I wanted this horse kept under wraps. You've got to remember, that the English partner who owned this horse wasn't back yet and had not signed the papers. So while I had possession of the horse, this guy could throw a monkey wrench into this sale and I could lose the horse. I didn't want to drive the horse before I knew the deal was sealed and the ink was dry. So after the horse qualified I decided to put the guy I bought the horse from on him and I instructed him on what I wanted him to do.

"Look, all I want you to do is to be dead last for most of the race and then at the very end, just move him up a little bit. In other words, don't show him up, just finish 5th, 6th, I don't care, as long as you maintain qualifying time."

"Sure, if that's what you want," he answered, not really sure why I was asking him to do this. Owners normally wanted to show everything a horse had.

Of course, everyone has a watch, so you know how fast each horse is going. So he sat dead last for most of the race and then he reached up and tapped Jet lightly and when he did, Jetlite shot forward and he missed winning that race by 4-5 inches. And now everyone at Freehold had seen what the horse did. We got Jet back to the barn and I was ripping mad.

"What were you doing, letting him go like that?" I demanded. "I told you to take it easy!"

The first words out of his mouth were, "Well you know, I didn't sell you no world champion! I didn't think he could do anything! I barely touched him and he took off!"

"That's fine, but now you've blown all of our betting money," I said with disgust.

Back in those day's we could have bet with bookies and won back all the money we paid for the horse. I was very aggravated. But I was more worried because here is this horse, and the papers are not signed yet, and if the other owner hears what the horse did, he could very well decide to keep him and race him himself. And there wouldn't be a darn thing I could do about it.

So I asked this owner who made the deal with me when the other owner was coming in and he told me that it would be later that same day. Well, I got the papers and I stood by the drivers entrance and when I saw him I ran up to him and told him that I had bought one of his horses, Jetlite from his partner and would he please sign the papers.

"Oh sure," he said. And without a hesitation he signed! I was so relieved and now I didn't care who told him what. Jet was mine! My heart was pounding like crazy.

So we went on with Jet and we won the next seven or eight races with him. We never pushed him he just went.

Each race he came up a second or two faster. Now it was time to go to Florida. Pompano had always been our destination in the winter. I approached my wife and we talked about what we were going to do now that we had this horse. We made a decision and sold our house, and we bought a mobile home in Pompano, which we intended to use for three months out of the year to live in and work out of when we wintered.

I took Jet to the track and had to qualify him all over because of Florida state regulations. This young fellow came over to me. His name was Clint Warrington, Jr. His father had worked for Stanley Dancer and had taken care of Stanley's horse, Dancer Hanover, and had ridden him in some races. Dancer Hanover was Jetlite's sire.

"You know my daddy rode this horse's sire and I would give anything in the world to set behind him just one time."

I knew this young man only had a "P" license at the time which means he couldn't drive on Saturdays, Sundays or holidays, just during the week. You need 150 Provincial drives before you can step up to an "A" license that allows you to drive anytime. But I could see how much this meant to the kid.

"I'll tell you what I can do. I'm going to drop you in the box, and list you as the driver but you've got to train this horse one time for me when I tell you and where I tell you without anyone knowing."

He agreed and so we waited until no one was around and across the street there was a big track. On our side was a 5/8 track, but this one was a mile. I jogged the horse over, and there was a couple of people I saw, but they didn't pay any attention to what I was doing. The kid was waiting for me, and who should be standing at the rails with him, but Stanley Dancer! Stanley had a big stable and he was one of the best drivers in the world. He had Albatross, and some other big time horses. He trained for the owner of Yonkers Raceway. He was the head trainer. I mean this guy was really well known. And I have known Stanley for years. But this day, Stanley was silent. He never said a word to me.

I took Clint aside and said, "Now look, here is how I want you to train this horse: In the last quarter you just reach up and tap him and let him go. I don't know how fast he can go, but just let him go."

So Warrington goes the first quarter in about 30 seconds and then he backs into Jet a little and taps him and that horse came around the last quarter in 27 seconds! I had to look at my watch twice to make sure I was seeing right. And then I look over at Stanley and he has a look of disbelief on his face, but he doesn't say anything.

I call Warrington back in and I asked Stanley what he thought.

"My God, I don't believe what I just saw. What kind of a horse is that?"

"I don't know. This is the first time ever let him go. We've won seven in a row just hanging on to him. We never let him go wide out. I have no idea what he can do."

Stanley just shook his head.

Well, we get the horse to the next race and Clint Warrington is driving.

"How do you want me to do this?" he asks.

"When the man says go, just reach up and touch him one time, get him to the front of the line and just cut the mile. If they beat you, they beat you. If you win, you win. I don't care. It don't matter to me one but, because he's young and he has a long time to race."

So he did exactly what I said. He went right to the front, and my God this horse is relaxed and just jogging away. No one can come close to him. Warrington gets down to the three-quarter pole, and he reaches up and taps him again and he wins that race. This colt that had never done more than 2:04, 2:05, wins this race in 1:59. We were all astounded.

That horse got written up in every magazine in the country. Nobody could believe that this 'P' driver had won this race in record time with this horse. No horse until that time had ever broke 2:00! After the race I looked over and Stanley was standing in the driver's section and he gives me the thumbs up. He had the biggest smile on his face, and I realized then that he had laid his money down on the Jetlite. He had clocked him at the same time I had the week before and that was with a jog cart! He knew immediately that this horse had what it takes. And he cashed in. I felt good about that.

We went on and raced this horse until he was twelve years old. A lot of people tried to buy him from me. In fact that first winter we had him in Pompano, one of the top people in the business at that time, came over to me and said he would give me $50,000 for Jetlite.

"You know, he's a four-year-old," I laughed. "I can still race him in New Jersey one more year. I'll make $50,000 just in stake races and that doesn't count the over-nighter's."

"You really think he is that good?" he asked.

"I know darn well, he is! You watch; he'll win all the stake races."

We went on to New Jersey that year and I went to the race secretary and told him I was in all the stake races.

"We got some really good horses this year, and I don't know if this horse is going to fit in with them or not," he said.

"Aw, don't worry about him, he'll be all right."

We won every stake race except one that year! And that was against the best horses in the state of New Jersey. After that, Jetlite was well known and we could go anywhere in the country. We would tell the race people we were bringing Jet and they'd tell us we could have anything we wanted. They'd bed him down with thick straw, big white bandages on him; he was like a star to them.

We set a track record in Maryland that held for four years. That's where they race the best horses in the country so that was a real honor for us. We were faster than anyone else had ever been on that track. In Maine we won the 1980 Presidential Race, which is the most prestigious race in New England, and they gave me a 6 ft. 6 inch trophy! Lloyd Johnson, General Manager at Scarborough Downs in Maine wrote about Jetlite shortly before the Presidential race. In the article, posted in the Sunday, August 17, 1980 race program, he wrote:

"The local favorite Jetlite will take another crack at that elusive 'sub-2:00 minute' barrier in this event, and is expected to take the field to a very fast early-clocking once the wings of the gate close. He tuned up for the race with a fine second place finish at Foxboro Raceway last weekend, pacing his last quarter mile in .28 seconds flat in a mile in 2:00 flat."

We also won the Durango, which was the second biggest race in New England.

Tragedy struck right before the Presidential race, when somebody set my barn in Scarborough, Maine, on fire and we lost everything. $440,000.00 worth of equipment, our horses, everything. It was devastating. I hired a kid for $250 a week because I felt sorry for him. He told me he had a wife and four kids and needed money to bring them down from north Maine. He had been working for Billy Parker, Jr., a friend of mine, and came to me and asked if I had extra work for him. I hired him and for a while he was doing a good job. He cleaned stalls and things like that. Well a few weeks later at 4:00 in the morning my barn was on fire. I could hardly believe it. We lost more than I can tell you. We tried to save the horses, but they wouldn't come out of the barn. If you can get them out and don't shut the door fast enough, they run back in. It is heartbreaking to watch something like that. It really tore me up. All my babies were gone.

Can you imagine? All the years and work I had put into those horses and it all went up in smoke and was gone in less than 30 minutes! You just never forget something like that.

After our fire, the same kid set 4-5 more fires before they finally caught him. He turned out to be a pyromaniac. The other barns he worked for had cameras and that is how they caught him. I don't know what eventually happened to him, but our losses were unbelievable.

And to make matters worse, a few days later when I sifted through the ashes my anvil was gone! The one thing I could use to make some money had been stolen. Well, I found it a short time later at some other guy's barn. When I questioned him he said he "found" it. I was hopping mad.

"Yeah, I'll bet. It just sprouted legs and walked away from my burning barn!"

I carried it out of there thinking how could anyone come and steal something from someone who had just lost everything? Guess some people just don't care.

Lucky for us, Jetlite just happened to be in Foxborough, Maine with my friend and driver Bucky Day. Thank God because he is the one who put us back on our feet again. We raced him and got most of our money back. But the hurt stayed with us for a long time. You don't get over something like that.

During the time after the fire, Jetlite really performed and we got back a lot of the money we had lost. This horse was phenomenal. He won race after race. His career as a racehorse paid off big when we entered him in the Presidential race. That day is one Marilyn and I will never forget.

The owner of the track decided he didn't want me to drive that day. I had four horses entered. He wanted Marilyn and I to sit up with him in the grandstands. He said he liked my horses a lot and said he knew we had the best stable on the grounds. He wanted us to be his guests. Marilyn was not real happy because she always tended to our horses herself before the races and she had a certain way of doing things.

Well, that day she gave specific instructions to the grooms and they did end up doing a good job.

At any rate, Bucky Day was my usual driver for Jetlite and he was scheduled to drive that day, but then he got called to Canada to drive in a big race. There was no way in the world that we figured Bucky could make it all the way from Canada to the race that day, since he had a late race the night before. So I put another guy down to drive the horse.

Well, when Bucky heard that he got so aggravated that he went and rented a car and drove all night long to get to the racetrack! He arrived 10 minutes before the race was to start. He called the race secretary immediately.

"I'm driving Jetlite," he told her.

"We have another driver down to drive," she answered.

"I don't give a damn who you have down, I'm telling you I am driving that horse!" he insisted. "I trained that horse, and no one else is going to drive him!"

The change was made.

Now the horse that Stanley Dancer owned named My Bill Forward was also entered in that race. For three or four days prior to the race, the newspapers had done several write-ups that no one could beat this horse. In fact, the horse was mentioned in the same article that Lloyd Johnson wrote about Jetlite:

"Another definite starter will be Maine's fastest two-year-old of all time, the great My Bill Forward, who stepped over the Bangor oval in 2:04.1 last summer. He has since moved on to the Meadowlands in New Jersey, and is currently one of the top three-year-olds in the rich New Jersey Sires Stakes program. He has shown a liking for a half-mile oval, and returned a winner in 1:58.2 at Freehold Raceway two weeks ago. His regular driver Donnie Dancer will be here for the big event."

Well, Bucky's brother-in-law Charlie just happened to have a horse that could really leap. No one could beat him out of the gate. He had the inside of My Bill Forward. Now I am not saying that he and Bucky connived anything but I personally think they made a deal and Charlie was going to park Dancer's horse. And Bucky was going to take advantage of that.

Now that day was raining real hard and it was a muddy mess. And when you get parked on the outside, I am telling you it is near impossible to get out of. The horse has to use a lot more strength to work through that mud, you know.

So sure enough, Charlie put the hammer down and he parked Dancer's horse and of course everyone else was at My Bill Forward's back so there wasn't anywhere he could go. Charlie took his horse down to the first half so fast no one knew what was happening. Now was time for Bucky to make his move. When he came around to the 5/8th and straightened out after the curve, he reached out and put the leather to that horse and that horse went full out right around Dancer's horse and everyone else. At the next curve, I held my breath. I knew there was a big hole coming up and I figured if he hit it at the speed he was going it would be all over. But Bucky was smart. He knew about the hole too. After all, he had raced there many times and he knew that course inside and out. Well, just before he hit that hole, he turned that bike to the inside and missed the hole and pulled away and won that race.

We were laughing our sides off in the stands. We won $10,000 that day which we needed badly. We had just lost everything in the fire and Bucky knew that. The owner of the track was happy too. He told us after the race that he won a fortune off that race. He had bet everything on Jet! He knew a good horse when he saw him!

Jet's Presidential trophy is still at the racetrack today.

Now before you think we had a push-button horse to begin with let me tell you a little bit about Jetlite. All was not smooth running with Jetlite at first. That horse was lazy as all get-out! We were having trouble getting him off to a fast start at the gate. At the time I had a friend named Eddie Taylor. Eddie's nickname was Fast Eddie. He could be a bit on the shady side at times, but he was a good guy. Well, he had this vet friend, Dr. Chase. Chase really liked Jetlite. He thought he was the best looking horse he had ever seen. So every day he would come over to my barn to see him. Well, I explained the problem I was having at the gate and he said he could fix that.

So the next day Eddie and Dr. Chase showed up at my barn with a broom handle, 2 horseshoe nails and an extension cord with the end cut off of it. We put the horse in cross ties in a big stall.

"What are we doing with this stuff?" I asked, a little puzzled.

"Just drive those two nails in the broom handle about a half inch apart," he explained. "Then take one of those wires and attach it to each nail and plug it in! And then stand far enough behind the horse so you don't get kicked and when I holler, 'HAA!' I want you to touch him in the rear with those two nails heads."

"You'll kill him! That's 110 volts!" I said stunned.

"No, not at that distance. All it'll do is shock him a little," the doctor assured me.

So I stood way back and old Doc said to get ready.

"When I holler you touch him."

"What if we kill him?" This was a good horse, and I didn't want him dead!

"We ain't going to kill him, but we will teach him to leave out of the gate!"

Well, he hollered and I lightly touched Jet's rear end and that horse just about broke the chains. I thought he'd kick my head off! And after that if a driver hollered "HAA" or just toughed him lightly with the whip that horse took off like lightening!

Up to that point we couldn't qualify him. He just wouldn't go and he did stupid things. He was just being a dumb colt. Well, after that jolt he got he ran and never stopped after that.

That horse won just about every race he entered. People couldn't believe it. He won us a ton of money.

In 1979, there was this one guy, Eddie Davis. He was out to win the driving championship for New Jersey that particular year. He was from Maryland. Him and Hervé Filion were fierce competitors. One race he would be on top and then the next Hervé would be in the number one spot. It went back and forth like that all the time.

Well, he came up to me one night and he said, "Ray, I'm trying to win as many races as I can and I've never had a chance to drive Jetlite. Do you think you could put me down on him for a race?"

"I tell you what I'll do, I'll put you down. I really don't want to see Hervé win against Jet anyway!" I answered with a laugh.

Eddie was a big guy, not your typical driver. But he was darn good. So he drives Jet and they win. And that year he won the driving championship. When he drove Jet it was only two days from the end of the season, so he won it just in time.

Eddie was a good friend. I remember one time when there was a mishap with one of my horses, Number Won Son that I had just purchased from Eddie. It was the first night I owned that horse. I bought him right before the race, but no one knew it. Another driver was driving the horse that night. His first name was Jackie. I went to him and explained the situation.

"Look Jackie, between you and I, I just bought this horse. Not officially, because Eddie still owns him, but as soon as this race is over he'll be paid and he's mine. But tonight I get the purse money. If you win tonight I'll make it worth your while. Instead of the normal 5%, I'll pay you 10%."

"Well, hell, I intend to win whether you pay me or not!" Jackie laughed.

Jackie's dad was a good friend of mine. In fact I watched Jackie win his first race on TV in his dad's kitchen. And he also dated my daughter, so he was like family.

So that night Jackie won the race, which paid $10,000. The $30,000 price for the horse now just cost me $20,000. So in the next race I decided to drive him. Well, this kid from Maine, who was known to have a cocaine problem, was driving on the outside of me. He didn't even realize I was on the rail. He came right up under my horse, hit him in the leg and crippled the horse. Here I had just paid all this money and the horse was injured because of some kid who was high.

Needless to say, I was pretty angry. And that is a nice way of saying it. After the race I walked into the drivers room and when got in there, I saw him slumped over in a chair. I grabbed a pool stick and went up to him and poked him in the leg. When he looked up I let him have it.

"You ever do that kind of stuff to me in another race and I'm going to break both of your legs and both of your arms. And don't think I wouldn't do it. I grew up really rough and I had to fight for everything I had, and believe me it wouldn't bother me a bit to hurt you bad."

Well, Eddie was in the room at that time and heard what I said.

"Aw, Ray, maybe he didn't mean it."

Lucky for me, another driver, Carmine stood up and said, "Eddie, I was right behind them in the race, and Ray is right. We could have all been killed tonight. If Ray had not really held on to that horse the whole field would have went down. And I ain't getting killed over some stupid kid on cocaine."

That kid went on to drive some more but eventually they took his license away. And this kid had it good. Back in Chicago he drove for my friend, and was making over $200,000 a year plus his percentage and he threw it all away for cocaine.

Back to Jetlite's story: After twelve years of racing we wanted him retired, to race no more. He would go out a champion. I was offered $35,000 for him, but refused. I didn't want anyone else racing him and possibly ruining him. He deserved better than that. We donated him to the police department. You could ride that horse, and do anything with him. He was the gentlest horse you'd ever seen. My grandson Regean, as a four-year-old youngster, used to go right in the stall, brush him, and that horse would stand still and never move. But we made him that way.

You see we didn't train like conventional trainers. As I said earlier, we had raced ponies before we raced horses. There were eight world champions in the world, and we happened to own seven of them! We could not get the eighth one because the owner would not sell her for any amount of money. She was the fastest mare in the world and nobody could beat her. This guy didn't have a lot of money, but he wouldn't part with her. He just loved racing. Her name was Miss Afton Direct. That is the only one we didn't have. We owned some fantastic horses, though. Horses like Curtis Bignoise, a 44-inch tall pony, and Charlau's Madonna Racey.

I have to tell you that out of all the horses we had, Curtis Bignoise really stands out. He was so mean, I mean you'd get in the cart behind him and you'd put your life on the line! He'd just as soon kick you in the face! And bite and strike at you! He was a mean little sucker. We used to have to put him in the trailer and chain him up as tight as we could before we could move anyone else in there. We didn't dare put him in after the others, because he would eat them up on his way in! (laugh) He wasn't very tall, less than 44", but man he was mean! I'd be racing him and he'd be reaching over trying to bite the horse next to him. Really, going full speed and I'd have to whack him with the whip to get his attention away from biting the other horses. And that little sucker didn't care!

But believe it or not, everyone loved him. He just did things his way. Now, Curtis Bignoise was the sire of Dr. Curtis and Lee Volo. They turned out to be the two fastest trotters in the world at that time. Dr. Curtis broke the world record and then I took it away from him. And that was kind of a scandal. What happened was that Dr. Curtis got too tall to race. So his owners took him down to the University of Pennsylvania and they cut his withers down so he could measure under the required height of 50". And then they entered him in the race. I drove Lee Volo in that race. Well, to begin with he wasn't as good as Lee Volo was, so they had to put heavier shoes on him to race. Now my shoes were as thin as a piece of aluminum. And using those shoes, Lee would trot just as fast as the wind! He didn't need the extra weight.

No one ever was able to prove that Dr. Curtis had been altered, but he was now a black horse with a big white stripe over his withers, and it hadn't been there before. After the race, it didn't really matter though. I knew I could take the track record away from him and that is exactly what I did. So in the end that owner lost his record and in my eyes, his honor. You don't do things like that.

Ray Smith on left Jet Lite Driver Eddie Davis on right

Chapter 3

I look back now and realize how many times I came close to death. People think that you just get behind a horse and run a race and that you are perfectly safe. That is not the case at all! In fact, you risk your life each and every time you get out on that track. Take for instance the time I raced at Freehold and took a bad spill. I believe it was June of 1986. This was just one of many injuries. Here is what the newspapers reported the day after the race:

"Harness driver, Ray Smith, 46, was being treated at a Freehold area hospital yesterday after being injured in the first race at Freehold raceway. He was reported to have a fractured vertebrae and possible internal injuries. Smith, driving Show Me the Way, was thrown to the track when Marvel Us went off stride and collided with his driver. Joe

Schwind, driving Kingsway Duke, trying to avoid Smith, pulling his horse sharply to the right but one of the sulky wheels passed over Smith. Schwind, 27, also was thrown to the track suffering a bruised hip and minor abrasions. None of the horses were hurt."

I guess I never really gave much thought to the dangers. I just drove and whatever happened, happened. When we were breaking all the records that was my only focus. Some of the other injuries I suffered left me with seven herniated discs, chips out of my right shoulder, a ruptured kidney, and a broken sternum. All the ribs on one side have been broken, I have been kicked in the face, had my teeth kicked out and capped, (in fact I don't breathe out of one side of my nose, but I do okay), two massive head concussions, a broken right leg, but nothing major. (laugh) Well, actually I DOA'd twice at the same hospital. But as you can see, they brought me back. Guess I'm pretty tough.

When you've done the things that I've done, like riding bulls and bucking horses when I was young, I never worried about getting hurt, and that's the honest truth. Getting hurt is all part of doing the things you love to do. You know the dangers before you go into it. It isn't "if" you're going to get hurt, it's "when". I mean I lost some good friends to injuries. There was one fellow out in California who wanted me to go out with him one night. I didn't really feel like going out, so I used Marilyn as an excuse. Blamed it on the little lady, you know, (laugh). So later that night he was racing and the line on the left broke and he only had one line left, and he baled out and was killed.

Another friend, Billy Haughton, was racing a different time. We were at Yonkers Raceway. I was in a body cast and couldn't drive, so I was holding his horse while he changed the headpoles. During the race that followed, Billy's horse broke and the horse right behind him ran him over. It wasn't the other driver's fault. There was nothing he could do once Billy's horse broke. The accident bore a hole right through his skull and he died. You know when we first started driving we only wore silk hats. Well, after some of the accidents like Billy's, we went to a light bicycle helmet, and then to a better one, and continued on until we got to what they wear today.

It was kind of strange because the night before the accident, my friend Carl Allen and I were talking with Billy. Billy was getting a horse ready for a race, a horse that was not a first class horse. Carl asked him why he was taking jobs with horses that were junk horses in his opinion, and Billy replied that if he didn't accept all the jobs that owners were offering him, they wouldn't call on him again and he would lose his paycheck. The next night he lost his life. That haunted me for a long time.

Immediately after the accident I had another race to run. Although emotion could have taken over, when you are a driver you have to put everything aside and do your job. I could have fallen apart that night, but I had to fight my feelings, and concentrate on the race. It's just the nature of the sport. Grieving came later, but has no place on the track, for your safety and that of the other driver's.

Author's note: In his harness racing career, William (Billy) R. Haughton examined more yearlings and with more detail than any other driver/trainer in history. He understood that paying attention to even the most minute detail would bring his owner's the best horses available and after all this job was his bread and butter, so he took it very seriously. Confirmation, gait and breed were his main objectives, but he was also adept at spotting even the most remote flaws. In a short time, he gained the respect of owners. They trusted him to buy the best horses at the best price.

He also had an advantage over other trainers because he had the ability to pay for a horse himself if none of the owners wanted it, and he would race it himself under his own name. He made sure he always had enough financing so that a good horse would not be passed up. At times, though his decisions may have hindered his moneymaking ability. Take for instance, the time in Kentucky when he purchased a colt that he really liked. There was a possibility of a knee problem, but Billy was convinced it would not hinder his racing ability. When he approached the owners, they turned him down, it looked like he was going to have to keep the colt and race him himself. He had paid more than he usually did, buying the horse for $19,000.

The next day, though, another trainer, Ralph Baldwin asked about the colt. Billy explained his suspicions about the colt's knees and offered the horse to the trainer for a $25,000 option. The trainer agreed and that colt went on to win $4,868,955! Billy was out a ton of money, but that is how the race business is.

Billy Haughton won more money (over $11 million) and more races (2800+) in his driving career than any other driver in history. Born on Nov. 2, 1923, he began driving as a child of 8. By the time he was a teenager, he was grooming at county fairs, and training horses during his summer vacations. He drove in his first race at 17 and registered his first win at 18. In 1958 he was voted Harness Horseman of the Year.

Billy died in July of 1986 in the racing accident at Yonker's Raceway in New York described above by Ray. The news of Billy's death dealt a severe blow to the Harness racing world. He will always be remembered as the greatest driver ever.

Incidentally, the son of Hall-of-Famer Billy Haughton, Peter D. Haughton made his first competitive drive at 16. He won the race driving Dr. Dewars. In the eight-year career that followed, young Peter won 571 races and more than $6 million in purses. He was especially successful in big stake races, taking The Roosevelt International twice with Cold Comfort in 1978 and with Doublemint in 1979; The Dexter Cup and The Zweig with Cold Comfort and The Prix d'Ete with Armbro Omaha. In the 1976 Kentucky Futurity, he spoiled his father Billy's Triple Crown bid with Steve Lobell by nosing him out in the fourth heat with Quick Pay. Unfortunately, Peter Haughton lost his life in an automobile accident in 1980 at the young age of 25, another terrible loss for the racing world.

Ray continues:

People come up to me and say, "You know, you should have written all of this down." My answer was simple.

"What difference would it make? That and fifty cent gets you a cup of coffee!" (laugh).

You know, I don't even have any of my trophies anymore. One was over 6 ft. tall! But we moved around so much, where were we going to put them? So I threw them out! Guess I should have kept some of them, but hey, I wasn't in racing for that. I was in it to make money. The only thing I kept was the shoeing box my uncle gave me when I first starting shoeing horses, my first anvil, and I kept my farrier apron. Other than that, nothing was saved. We didn't even take many photographs. That just didn't occur to us. This was our job, not something we went into for the glory.

Once you've done it, it doesn't matter. I don't have to tell anyone what I have done. (Although I guess that's what I am doing now!) (laugh) I know what I did, and I'm happy with the things I accomplished and that is all that matters. I wasn't the best driver, far from it. I wasn't the best trainer either, but I came up with innovations that they are still using today that nobody else did!

Take for example, this story. I had a friend named Eddie Cobb, who owned Ghingas Kahn, one of the top horses in the world. I went to Eddie and asked if I could breed one of my mares to Ghingas Kahn, or I wanted a colt from the horse. He looked at me and sort of laughed.

"I've bred him to five or six mares and I am not sure what he is going to produce. I don't really have him up for stud to the public yet."

He told me that he had another colt out at his farm that I could look at. He was trying to eliminate some of the horses because he had been diagnosed with cancer. So I took another owner I knew with me and as we were watching the colt out in the field, this horse, a nice looking guy, is trotting up a storm. Now he was pacing bred so he wasn't supposed to be trotting. Man, he was something to see! Head up, tail in the air, he was beautiful. So I asked to have him brought in and I checked him out and decided to buy him. I paid Eddie $10,000, and brought him home. I named that colt Eddie Khan after my friend.

We took the colt down to Pompano, to break him, because he was a yearling. I put a set of hobbles on him and he nearly killed me in the stall! He reared up, kicked at me, pawed at me, bit at me, boy, he was angry! "Whoa," I thought, "What am I doing wrong?" I had been gentle with him and he had no reason to come at me like that. I called some people to come over to give me a hand and we dressed him up again. It took three of us to get him out of that stall. He was mad as hell.

I hooked him up to a jog cart and took him down to the training track right by out barn. I took him out on the track and that darn horse ran me right through the middle of the track, broke the jog cart off, and tore up the equipment I thought, "Holy cow, what am I going to do with this horse?"

So I decided to take all the shit off of him, and put a harness on him. If he wants to run, I'm going to let him run, if he wants to gallop, he can. I'm going to let him go until he decides he wants to be a racehorse. So what does he do? He starts trotting! I thought, "Wait a minute, this guy was sired by a world class pacer. He isn't supposed to be a trotter!"

I knew then that if anyone put hobbles on him, he would hurt them. Put a harness on him however, and he was the gentlest horse you've ever seen! So I raced him in some stake races and he did well. But I could never let him just go. He'd make a break just like that. He had so much power.

Then an idea came to me. I said to Marilyn, "Do you remember when we raced ponies? What did we do with a pony when we wanted to trot and he wanted to break?"

"We put trotting hobbles on him."

Well, the race people never heard of this. They use pacing hobbles, which are different. Well, I took a pair of the pacing hobbles, that go around their front legs, and put a rope between them and attached a pulley in the middle of his belly with a loose strap so it won't fall down, and I hooked two lines back to the cart. Now the rope goes through that pulley and when the left foot goes forward, the left foot has to go back. It gives the horse support. You see ponies are not gaited like the big horses. You have to teach them to trot. This devise worked perfect for that. They could still go into a canter, but it did teach them the correct gait.

So I am at the Meadowlands with the horse and I meet up with this old trained named Howard Beissinger, who was a world-renowned trainer. He was a real cowboy. Well he came along side of me and caught my attention.

"Hey, kid, what the hell you got on that trotter?"

"I got trotting hobbles on him," I replied.

"What the hell are they?"

"Well, when we raced ponies we used to do this for horses who wanted to make a break. This horse has a powerful amount of speed and he'll make a break in a heartbeat. With these, I can control his gait."

"I've been in the business for a long time, but that's the damndest thing I ever seen in my life," he said. "Do they work?"

I just laughed.

"Yes sir they do. They won't keep a horse from breaking if he really wants to, but they steady him. He can gallop if he wants to but they really make a difference in his gait."

I went ahead and raced this colt, Eddie Khan, in a stake race and he was doing well. I was in for $100,000, and when another driver at the end of the stretch bumped me, it knocked Eddie sideways. I had the rail and didn't lead, so everybody passed us and I was dead last. I managed to get him to the outside because I knew he would relax and he did. He started going and one by one he knocked each horse off until we were in a position to win, when the horse in the second position made a break, hit me and knocked me into the middle of the racetrack, I finished third. I was sick, just sick at heart. But things like that happen. The main thing is that the hobbles worked and this horse was going to be a moneymaker.

In fact this colt turned out to be fantastic. Later my dear friend Eddie was in the hospital dying, and after I had qualified the horse and we won a race, I called him on the phone.

"Guess who just won today?" I asked.

"Who?" he answered weakly.

"Eddie Khan! You should have seen him. He trotted like a world champion! I was so proud of him."

Eddie was thrilled. I knew how much that meant to him. Sadly it was the last time I ever got to talk to my good friend. Eddie Cobb died shortly after that.

Author's note: Howard Beissinger, mentioned above, took a 3-year old named Tarport Lib and made her the fastest pacing mare in the history of the sport. Beissinger won with a time of 1:56 2/5. Tarport Lib came out of two pacing crosses: sire, Thorpe Hanover and dam, Adios Betty.

Chapter 4

People sometimes ask me who was responsible for getting us into the big time in harness racing. Well, that person is John McNamara. Do you recognize that name? Well when I first heard it, I didn't know either. I was racing in New Jersey one evening, and I happened to be sitting with John's trainer and we got to talking. He pointed over to where John stood talking to someone, and asked me if I knew who that was.

"No," I answered.

"That's John McNamara," he said.

"Who the hell is John McNamara?" I said, the name not familiar.

"M&M!" he said, looking at me like I was nuts!

"M&M what?" I retorted. It never dawned on me that he was talking about M&M candy.

"You dummy, M&M candy! The M&M stands for McNamara and Mars (Mars Candy Company). John is the man who invented M&M's."

"Aw bull-shit," was all I could say. "What's he doing here?"

"He's going to drive ponies tonight. That's what he does for fun," the driver continued.

Well, that night I was introduced to John and he took a liking to me and he knew I was a friend of his trainer. Over the years John and I became good friends as well. In fact we never bought candy for our kids after that. John kept them supplied with M&M's! He'd bring them over to the kids by the bagsful!

One time John had his trainer Whitey Wardluft and I come down to his 3500-acre property in Virginia. It happened to be right next to Arthur Godfrey's home! Remember him? It was one hell of a property. I remember when John's daughter got married; they used Madonna Racey, a pretty famous horse at the time, and another white stallion, to pull a carriage to the ceremony.

You get to meet a lot of famous people when you drive in the big races, and are known for your horses, like we were. John McNamara used to hob-knob with Jackie

Kennedy-Onassis! I would go with one of John's trainers to saddle up two huge Belgium Draft horses he owned. Just massive horses! At least 17 hands, the kind of horses you needed a ladder to mount! Anyway, John would ride these Belgium's with Jackie O. I saw her at the ranch many times when she would come to fox hunt.

I even got to meet Minnesota Fats! I actually played pool with him! Well not exactly, I shot one ball and he cleared the table. (laugh) We also met Tiny Tim. That didn't turn out so well though. I would rather have not met him! What happened was that I happened to be racing that night and Tiny Tim was at the microphone singing. I had a little filly who had not raced before and it was nighttime. I figured I would warm her up before the race, and Tim had that ukulele he was always playing, and just as I passed by him he hit that real high note in the song, "Tip Toe Through The Tulips", and that filly spooked and went left, right over the hub rail, and the next thing I knew, we went flying over a big ditch and she kept on going, with me hanging on for dear life. There also happened to be a big alligator pond right along the side of the ditch, and I was so sure we were going right in it! But that filly headed back to the barn instead. Whew! Yep, you can say that Tiny Tim was not my favorite person that night, that's for sure. It was hysterical later, but not that night. I was mad as hell.

Another thrill for me was when I got to meet Bea Farber. I always thought she was the most exceptional woman driver I had ever seen in my life. She went around the world competing with the best, most well known men drivers. At the time they were paying her $5000.00 a day to go on this tour. I had so much respect for her. I always enjoyed talking to her at Pompano.

Author's note: First working as a secretary in a lawyer's office, Bea Farber made an impact on the world of harness racing like no other woman in history. Retiring in 1995 with more than 1800 winners under her belt, her list of accomplishment's are impressive.

Born and raised near Port Huron, Michigan, Bea was always around horses. She began her driving career in 1970 when she was tired of working in an office and wanted something more out of life. Being married to a horseman, she gravitated back to horses and soon entered the harness racing world.

From her first driving title in 1973, she paved the way for women in harness racing and became its first female superstar. Bea competed both in the United States and Internationally and in 1976 she represented the USA in defeating the European drivers and later won the Italian International Driving Championship in Florence, Italy.

Bea was named Sportswoman of the Year for the March of Dimes in 1980. From 1978 through the 1980's she resided in Florida and in 1982, she was the leading percentage driver at Pompano Park with a UDR of .368. Her most memorable horses at Pompano included Quick Harry, Quick Command and Quick Candy.

Bea retired in 1995 completing 9,621 races with 1801 wins and earnings of just over $9 million. She has been written up in People's Magazine, Vogue and the Wall Street Journal and appeared on many television shows promoting the sport. The U.S. Trotting Association asked her to help make a film in 1980 entitled, "Queen Bea", featuring her racing success. It was shown around the United States, especially on airplanes.

When interviewed in 2007, Bea admitted to a pinched nerve in her lower back, a rotated hip, and a replaced knee from being thrown out of harness racing carts. And she has troublesome arthritis from years of gripping the reins to control those powerful animals. She likens it to getting in fifty car wrecks in your lifetime! Her last bad accident was in 1994. The horse flipped her out of the buggy mid-race, and she flew ten feet and was trampled by other horses in the race. One horse's knee actually dug into her back, causing a few ribs to break in half!

When Bea quit racing, she gave up everything related to her old life. Currently she walks 2 miles, and bikes 10 miles every morning and says she is in the same shape she was at age 22. She also ballroom dances five night a week! Bea added a dimension to the harness racing world that will not soon be forgotten. Some of her records still stand!

Ray continued:

Over the years we came across so many wonderful people. One of them was G.C. Hillenbrand. His family owned Hillenbrand's Casket Company in Batesville, Indiana. G.C. was the richest man in Indiana at the time. He was quite a man. Did you know that he was also a gourmet chef, and he cooked my dad's 50th birthday dinner? He sure did!

I remember G.C. coming to the races with his wife and he would pull me aside and say, "Can you take my wife around and introduce her to some of these people? You know more of them than I do."

And I would take her around and we'd talk to some of the wealthiest people in the business. She always got a kick out of that.

I could go on and on telling you about the people I met but the main thing is that racing gave Marilyn and I the opportunity to expand our world and experience so many things that we never would have known had we not been in harness racing.

I have to say though, that the person who taught me the most about racing was Stanley Dancer. I mentioned him earlier. That man knew more about racing than anyone I ever knew. He gave me the most help to learn the business. I didn't know a lot when I first started racing the Standardbreds. My experience had been with ponies. At the time, Stanley had a couple of brothers in the business too and he owned a place called Egyptian Acres. It was a beautiful place that even had a putting golf course! Well, I asked him if I could bring my ponies down to train.

"Mr. Dancer, I don't have a good place to train my ponies, I just have a farm track and it's not that good. Do you think I could use your track?" I asked.

"I don't use that empty barn down there anymore," Stanley replied pointing to another area of the property. "You can stall your horses in there and use anything you want."

He actually owned the sire to Jetlite, by the name of Dancer Hanover. So I brought my ponies to his property and used his track to train them. From that day on I followed Stanley around, watched him closely, questioned him and he was always willing to teach me whatever I wanted. I learned early on that there is so much to learn that you really cannot do it on your own. You need a network of people to teach you. Each person has his or her own something to add and if you pay attention you can pick up a lot of information that will help you in the long run. And that is what I did.

I'm going off the track for a moment to spend a little time on the importance of a good stopwatch. That is one of the main things I learned early on. But first let me explain licensing. Remember I mentioned earlier that one of the young drivers of mine had a "P" license? Well there is a reason for that. You see when the harness driver's association set up the rules many years ago, they designated the "P" license as a beginners or novice license. No driver can get a regular license until he has 150 provisional drives under his belt. That is in addition to 50 or 75 qualifying races before you can even get a "P" license. In other words, you don't just walk out there and say that you want to be a harness driver. No owner with an expensive horse is going to let some kid sit behind that horse without a lot of experience. So once you get your "P" license and have enough drives, then you can apply for an "A" license. They make it pretty tough. You also have to take a 3-hour test that quizzes you on every aspect of harness racing, equipment, rules etc. Once you pass that, then you are considered an "A" driver.

As I mentioned, the test is supposed to take about 3 hours. Well back when I took it, I had to go to Dover, Delaware. So I am sitting there, writing, writing, and writing. They told us beforehand that we needed to have every single rules memorized and boy did I study for that test. You cannot believe how many rules there are! Less than an hour after I began that test, I got up and handed the finished paper to the instructor.

"Don't you think you better go back over some of this stuff, son? It's a pretty hard test," the instructor asked, fearing that I had rushed through it and would fail.

"Naw, I knew most of it. It seemed pretty easy to me," I answered.

Now this was before I had all the head injuries of course, and back then I had a photographic memory. I could read something one time and I knew it. I didn't have to think about it, I knew it!

"You know you don't have to turn this in right now," the instructor insisted.

"I know, but I'm in a hurry to go home," I answered.

"Why don't you wait around a few minutes and I'll run through your paper to see how you did," he said.

So I did and I only got one damn thing wrong. Actually I knew the answer, but I wrote it down wrong. The instructor shook his head and said he had never seen anyone finish the test that quickly and get all but one answer correct.

"Well, you know I am pretty good at remembering facts," I said to him

"Pretty good? Hell, man you knew that test better than most I've seen!" he answered.

"Well, I want to drive horses pretty bad."

Most of the people who take that test sit there and try to figure out different things like what bit to use when. I can tell you every kind of a bit, and every kind of rigging there is. By the time I took that test, I just knew it. I was the kind of person who would listen and pay attention to these old men when they would talk to one another in the barns, and they were smart! One guy who was named to the Hall of Fame, Joseph C. O'Brien, was the leading person in the world as far as rigging. He was from Canada and could rig any kind of a bad horse. He just had a natural ability to know exactly what to put on a horse to get the best performance out of him.

I had a colt one time at the Meadowlands that I was having problems with. He was on the bit all the time and was just plain uncontrollable. He was irritated and I knew it but I didn't know what the problem was or how to correct it. So this particular day, Joseph O'Brien happened to be racing with me, which was unusual. He rarely came to the Meadowlands. He was Canadian and mainly raced there. And so I asked him, "Sir, I'm Ray Smith and I am sure you don't know who I am, but I am having a problem with my horse and I was wondering if you wouldn't mind coming over to check him out. I know that if there is anyone in the world that can help it is you."

"I do know who you are and I would be happy to look at the horse," Mr. O'Brien said. "Give me a couple of minutes and I'll be right over."

I told him what section I was in, and sure enough, a short time later he came over and closely examined the bridle I was using.

"I know the problem is with the bridle and I know I have it wrong, but I don't know how to fix it," I explained.

He adjusted it here and there and gave me some clues as to the type of bit I should be using. He told me to make a couple of changes, and adjusted the bridle and bit. That next race, the horse was a good 50% better. After that I changed to the bit that Mr. O'Brien recommended and boy that colt drove like a Cadillac!

That is the good thing about drivers. Even though we were racing against the other drivers, we helped each other. We didn't dislike one another. Our lives depended on looking out for each other. Think about it, if you don't get along with the drivers on a certain track and they get a chance to run over you, they will. You better learn to get along. I learned early on to say "yes sir", "no sir", and I minded my manners. You show respect and you'll get respect.

You know I have learned that there is always someone who knows a little bit more than you do. It is an ongoing education. You really need to be in the business for a good five years to learn what you need to know. And from there it takes experience and doing something every day until it becomes second nature. You just automatically do things. But that doesn't happen overnight.

That is why my friend Hervé Filion has won so many races (more about his racing career later). There isn't anyone who can hold a candle to him. He is phenomenal.

Okay back to the stopwatch. Most people don't realize how important a stopwatch is to the drivers. I don't know if you have ever seen a driver up close enough during a race to notice that stopwatch in his hand. If you don't know how to read the stopwatch while you are driving, you have a bad disadvantage in a race. Without it, you have no idea of how fast you are going. Because you can't always look at the timer, you'll pass it before it flashes. You have to depend on your watch.

When you train the horse, you don't take him out on to the track and just go. You clock him and gauge your distance and time with your watch. You already know for instance, that you want to go through the first quarter at 45 seconds. So you set your training schedule up according to that watch. I got so good at it, that say I wanted to go a 30-second quarter, I didn't even have to look at the watch after a while. When I got to that quarter, I was right on, within 1/5 or 2/5 of a second. It's just like when you drive your car. Once you are an experienced driver, you don't have your eye on the speedometer every second. You just know that you are going 50 or 65 mph. You just know! That is why knowing your stopwatch and learning how to properly use it will win you races. It is about the most important tool you will use.

Now on to how John McNamara got us into the big time. After Marilyn bought her first pony for $200, we heard about another one that was for sale. He was a champion Welsh pony that they wanted $3500.00 for. That was a lot of money back then. But we saved up and when we had the money I went to talk with the trainer. I asked him if the horse was really that good, and the man assured me that he was, although he had quarter cracks in his hooves. Since I shod horses, I wasn't worried about that, so I made arrangements to see him and Marilyn and I drove to Virginia. We pulled our horse trailer in a snowstorm, but we got there. It turned out to be John McNamara's ranch. It was an enormous 3500-acre spread with cattle and horses.

Well, we were taken to the stable and saw the horse for the first time. My God, he was a beauty. Long tail to the floor, snow white in color, silky beautiful mane, and big dapples on him. I knew I just had to have him. I checked out the feet and was convinced I could fix them. It was winter and I would have plenty of time to deal with it before the race season began.

We loaded the pony and drove back home to New Jersey. Shortly after that, I took him to the University of Pennsylvania and in those days we didn't know what we know today. We drilled holes in the feet and took piano wire and pulled the quarter crack together and put an acrylic overlay to hold it tight. We then added plastic shoes on this trotter. This was unheard of because normally they need weight in the front to make them trot.

When we started the season in the Meadows in Pennsylvania, that little pony shattered all the world records! Nobody could believe that a trotter could win with plastic shoes. And that the quarter cracks had been that bad. Between the farrier at the University of Pennsylvania and myself, we fixed it so the horse didn't hurt anymore. It may have been unconventional, but it worked! Once he wasn't in pain, that horse could fly!

Well, when John McNamara heard of the success we were having he was thrilled. Although he no longer owned the horse, he was very supportive. He knew the amount of work we had put into the horse and appreciated our efforts. We had picked up some other good horses along the way, mostly what we could afford. Mind you I was still just an electrician and didn't have a lot of money at the time. I had given up a tremendous job to begin as a harness driver.

About that time John called and told us about a sale he was going to have. All the top people in the country would be there. When John McNamara had a sale, people came! He was a very wealthy man and everyone knew the quality of his horses. He wanted me there for a week and put me up in his guesthouse.

"I want you to go out and inspect the horses before the sale and you decide what you want to buy. You can have any horse and as many of them as you want," John told me.

"John, I appreciate that but I can't do that. I am just an electrician and I don't have the money it would take to buy any of your horses," I told him honestly.

"I know that, but don't worry about the money. I don't care what they go for, if you see a horse you want, bid on him. I don't care how many you buy, just buy the best," John insisted.

"Well, how am I going to pay for them?" I asked.

"You let me worry about that," John replied.

"Okay, sir," I said, humbled that his man trusted me.

So the next day I go to the sale and I was so nervous. Every time you raise your hand in the auction, that's another $500. That was a huge deal for me. Well, I bought about six or seven horses that day. Turns out that John had already told the auctioneer that no matter what I bought, he should just put in on the books. After the auction ended, I went up to see how much money I owed, and the auctioneer told me not to worry, Mr. McNamara had already taken care of it.

I saw John the next morning at breakfast, and he was talking to the fellow who developed Virginia Beach. I didn't want to interrupt so I waited until they were finished talking and I approached John.

"Mr. McNamara, we need to figure out how I am going to pay you for these horses," I said.

"Why, are you worried about it?" he asked.

"Yes sir, I am. I pay my debts. Whatever it takes I will do it."

So John gets a table napkin and he wrote "I own John McNamara (so many thousands of dollars)" and he handed it over to me to sign.

"I still don't know how I am going to pay this off," I said, shaking my head.

"I tell you what, you go and race those ponies and when you win you just send me a little money here and there. I don't care how long it takes you to pay it off."

So that is what we did, and in six months time, we only owned him $400! I paid back every penny except for $400. John called me a short time after that and said he had a horse trailer he needed repaired. His horses had kicked the sides in and the plywood was getting bad and he really needed it rebuilt. I said no problem. So I went and picked up the trailer and took it to my shop, and I rebuilt that thing from top to bottom. I put the best of everything in it. When I took it back to him and he asked how much I owed him. I said nothing!

"Oh no," John said. "I realize what it cost to have a good trailer like this rebuilt."

"It doesn't cost anything to you," I insisted, knowing how good the man had been to me and how much trust he had placed in me.

"I'll tell you what then," John said. "You don't owe me that last $400. We'll just call it even. Our debt is clear. How's that?"

So I agreed to that. You know it was different back then. And this was a perfect example of that. In those days you just shook hands on a deal. There were no contracts. Your word had to be good because when you are in the racing business, they scrutinize you pretty well. I mean, if you ever lie to someone, or go back on your word they are not going to ever trust you again or cut you any breaks. John McNamara did not have to trust me like that. But he knew that when I said I would pay him back I would do just that. There was so much more honor then than there is today. You knew that you better not break your word.

Anyway, we took those ponies that we bought from John to the track the next year and we made enough money that we were able to keep buying the best horses money could buy. As I mentioned in an earlier chapter, in a short time we went from being small time harness drivers to owning seven out of the eight world champion USTPA (United States Trotting and Pacing Association) ponies. And I credit that to the faith John McNamara had in me.

Chapter 5

I've been asked how I started doing my horses feet. I didn't know a thing about shoeing horses until we got the ponies. Marilyn and I had 40 acres in New Jersey, and we built this huge barn. It was so big I could put 10,000 bales of hay in the loft. It was made of block walls. I mentioned earlier that the barn burned down. But before that I had a number of ponies stalled in that barn.

My uncle, by the name of Shirley Nielsen (yes his first name was Shirley!) was an old Danish cowboy, ten years to the minute and day older than me. I was born on July 31, 1939 at 1:30 in the afternoon and he had been born on July 31, 1929 at 1:30 in the afternoon! How is that for a coincidence?

All he ever did his whole life was work with horses and cattle. He worked for a big rancher in Louisiana. He could rope, and he could brand. He would take 2 year-old cows out, rope them, and doctor them right in the field. He was an old-timer who did things the old fashioned way.

Anyway, I had about 30 ponies and I needed someone to shoe them. I couldn't find anyone, and I really didn't know how to do it myself, so I bought a forge, (one of those old hand crank ones that ran on coal), some metal, half round, flat and grooved, and my uncle came and taught me how to work the metal from scrap, how to punch the holes in them, form and shape the shoes and how to shape the foot on the horse. He was an expert shoer. He could build any kind of a shoe and shoe any kind of a bad horse. I would follow around and watch him as he worked. He showed me how to use the anvil, heat the shoes, turn them and how to dress the hoof down, etc. We'd buy cold rolled steel and make our own shoes. In fact I mentioned that I still have the same anvil, shoebox and farrier apron. I keep teasing Marilyn that one of these days I'm going back to shoeing. She won't even let me near a horse anymore! (laugh) Once my uncle taught me what he knew I continued to shoe all of my horses.

My Uncle Shirley taught me a lot about doctoring horses too. I thought I knew a lot, but he knew so much more. He was one hell of a horseman. You take an old cowboy like him and they know more than any book can teach you. They grew up with horses and had experience you don't get from going to school.

As far as the shoes go, those shoes wear out very fast. My horses were shod every two weeks. I mean, think about it. They are racing just about every day; we exercise them daily, they put a lot of miles on those shoes.

Now that I look back at it, I was a better farrier than I was a driver, probably because I loved doing it. I put my heart into shoeing horses. People would bring me horses that no other farrier would touch. They were too hard to handle and sometimes downright dangerous. And these horses would stand there like babies for me. The owners were flabbergasted. But I had a way with horses. I talked to them, rubbed them, talked some more, and gained their trust. That was the key. I wasn't mean to them or domineering. I was gentle and they understood that. It was all in the handling. I showed no fear, and once I earned their trust, boom, boom, I would shoe them.

Occasionally I had a horse that would try to bit or kick me, but I held my ground, and once they knew I wasn't there to hurt them, they cooperated. I mean I had people paying me big bucks to shoe these horses. They didn't have anyone else that would put shoes on their horses so I was the one they came to.

I remember one horse though who was a real pistol. This guy could be a maniac. The owners needed him shod and I agreed to do it. But first I had to come up with a way to calm this fellow down. Well, it may have been looked on as abuse by some people, but I bent back one of his front legs and tied it up. Then I led him out of the stall to a long area leading out to the pasture. I ran this horse back and forth a few times and then changed legs and tied up the other one. Again, I ran him 3-legged. When that horse finally got back in the stall, he stood quiet like a baby while I put his shoes on. Sometimes you have to use unconventional ways to get the results you need. I didn't hurt the horse, just showed him who was boss. But this was for my safety, and not to be mean to the horse. Believe me horses can cause great injury.

On another occasion I was in a stall, and decided since we were short of time before a race that I would do a quick cleanout of the stall. My horse was not in the cross ties, but I figured he was calm and wouldn't be bothered. I grabbed the pitchfork and began to clean the manure when this horse reared and began kicking. He had me backed into a corner and I had no escape. Just about the third time his back feet whizzed past my head, I struck him hard with the pitchfork. It hurt him, but he was stunned enough that I could get the heck out of that stall. I could NEVER condone purposely injuring an animal, but when your life is at stake you have to react quickly. That was one of those times.

I truly enjoyed being a farrier more than I did driving. I loved the challenge of working with a difficult horse. Anyone could do a calm horse, but these hard horses gave me real satisfaction. Getting a horse to do what I wanted him to do left me with a good feeling. Take Jet Lite for instance. That horse had the ability, but no one could make him do anything. He was entered in the stakes as a two-year-old and again as three-year-old, but missed both of them because he wouldn't perform. At the time, New Jersey had decided to only allow four-year-olds compete for one more year. And Jet was very close to that age. After I worked with him, we entered him and he won everything! It was a matter of how we handled him.

Author's note: One evening when Ray and I sat at his dining room table talking I asked him what characteristics made a good jockey (driver). This was his answer:

First of all, the most important characteristic is integrity. The reason for that is that if you don't have integrity and you cheat the owner you are going to lose the owner and your income. That is why I never tried to tell an owner that a horse was better than he was. If the horse wasn't any good, I told him. I didn't tell him to leave him with me for another month like some trainers would do. I knew that man was in it to make money. So I think integrity is really important.

Honesty plays a role in integrity, too. I have seen too many cases where someone bought a cheap horse and turned around and told an owner that the horse was worth three times what it was really worth. Well, the horse didn't perform then, and that makes it bad for the industry. When I saw a horse at a sale, I would tell my owners what I thought the horse could do. If I didn't see potential, and they decided to buy it anyway, then at least I could say that I was honest. I couldn't tell an owner how to spend his or her money, but I could tell them if I thought the price was too high or if I thought the horse wouldn't be good in competition. I was always very honest with people and I think that sets you apart. Owners trust that you will do everything to make their horses win.

One more trait of a good driver is gentleness. That may seem silly, but horses respond better to a kind driver. You don't let them get away with anything, and you handle them with firmness, but there is no need for brutality. Trainers who beat their horses have no business driving. Beating a horse does not make it go faster. My idea has always been if you tap a horse two or three times and he doesn't respond, you aren't going to get much more out of him. Cutting him to pieces and making him bleed is so unnecessary. That doesn't get it in my book. I mean don't get me wrong, I have done it. If I have a horse who is acting up real bad and is kicking and such, I have laced him real good. But that is self-protection, and not doing it to be mean or get more speed out of him. Humane treatment gets better results.

Another attribute a good driver must have is confidence. You have to believe in yourself. You cannot show any fear during a race. If you are fearful, you are going to make a mistake and you are going to hurt somebody. If you are nervous, you have no business being in that bike. I don't care how bad you have been hurt before, once you are on that track you put all of that behind you. If you can't do that, you need to quit. Everyone on that track depends on the other drivers to be in good shape. They don't want to be out there if someone is not up to par. That is dangerous for everyone. One stupid mistake can injure or kill someone.

Taking good care of the equipment is also important for a driver. Your tack is only as good as the care that goes into it. Owners don't want inferior apparatus on their million dollar horses. That is one of the fastest ways to lose a job. A good driver keeps his tack in good shape and makes sure it is clean and no broken parts. Along with that comes the responsibility of knowing your equipment and how to use it. When it comes to rigging a horse, there wasn't a better person in the world than Joseph O'Brien. I had the privilege of learning from him and it stayed with me for my whole career.

Author's note: Joseph O'Brien, Canadian born, is a member of the Canadian Sports Hall of Fame and has won more races (2400 plus) than any driver with the exception of Billy Haughton. O'Brien began his career at the young age of 13 in 1930. He remains one of the biggest names in harness racing.

Ray and I switched subjects when I inquired about the innovations that have come up with over the years in harness racing. He continues:

In the old days, the harness was made out of wood. The bike seat sat up closer to the horse. Now they use metal and the seat is much further back. They don't use wood shafts anymore either. They cut the shafts off, and a guy who was later barred from racing, I don't recall his name at the moment, invented quick hitches. He gave them to a driver named Frank O'Mara. Frank is a great big guy, over 200 lbs. Frank said he was leery of trying the hitches because he thought they might come apart. So I said I would take them. Well, I went to Freehold, New Jersey and I tacked them right on to the harness, and I attached this device onto the shaft of the bike (cart). I put a safety hitch onto it and that is all I used to hold the horse. If the horse goes down you pop the pins out and the horse if free from the bike. None of this trying to undo straps etc. It is so much safer, not only for the driver, but the horse as well.

So I brought it to the track and the hitch was up about a quarter of an inch off the horses back, because you don't tighten the girth. You use a type of a breast collar that holds the harness to the back. I am the first person who ever used it and everyone at the track thought I was nuts. Well, it picked the horse right up and he flew! A friend of mine, Lucien Fontaine, watched this and came up to me after the race and asked if I would mind loaning him the set up.

"I heard you used this and had to see for myself. I'd really like to give it a try," he said.

"My owner has a machine shop and he made me five sets of them. Sure, Lucien, I'll loan you a set," I answered.

He took them and won race after race. From that point on, every driver used them. The metal shafts, (if they broke off would go straight through your belly), were replaced with this device and made it so much safer.

Another innovation I mentioned earlier was the trotting hobbles that I first brought to Meadowlands in New Jersey. If you watch now, in a race, three or four of the drivers will have on these same hobbles. It was something no one had every thought of doing but is used regularly now. Using those, we made trotters out of ponies that were never meant to trot. The hobbles allowed us to do that.

Author's note: Our conversation turned to the question of how drivers and vets are sometimes asked to do unscrupulous things to horses. Ray had some insight to this problem:

People will sometimes ask vets to do things that they shouldn't be asking. The vet knows that it isn't good for the horse, and that the owner is just looking for a big win. I never went to a vet and asked for anything that I wouldn't put into my own body. If it wasn't good for me, it wasn't going into that horse. I tell you I have seen some terrible things. Like putting bleach into a horse's veins to make him crazy and run like hell. I've seen them take pills and shove them into the horse's rectum to get it into his system quickly and make him go faster. It makes me sick. But when you are in the business, it is better to look the other way and keep your mouth shut. That is sad, but true. What other people do is their business. But the good side is that these people are going to get caught. The regulatory boards have their ways of checking horses and the power to deal with dishonest people. With the fines and suspension and the embarrassment, it just isn't worth it. If you can't do things honestly then don't do it! And that is where integrity comes in. As a trainer or driver it is up to you to say to the owners, "Look, I am not going to damage this horse." If you can't do that then you are not a person who should be in this business. I could have made a lot more money doing it the shady way. But at what cost to me? I would have lost face with the other drivers and damaged my credibility. Better to walk away and not deal with people of that caliber. Again, it isn't worth it.

I learned the hard way that it does not pay to drug a horse. And I was totally innocent, but it didn't matter. Here is what happened. I had a horse with the snots (that's what they called it back then). The vet I took him to in Maryland suggested giving a sulfur medication that was legal in Maryland and would help and would be out of his system in a week or two. I agreed and the med was administered.

Well, three weeks later I took the horse to an invitational race in Pennsylvania. So before the race the usual blood tests were given and the vet came to me and said he had to pull my horse from the race. Surprised, I asked why and he said that the horse had come up positive for drugs. I assured him that we had stood guard over the horse, and no one had got to him to give him anything. I was sure there was a mistake. The vet insisted the horse was drugged. I asked the vet if he could tell me what the horse tested positive for and he said it was the sulfur. I related the story of the Maryland vet and this vet said there was nothing he could do. A drug is a drug. I insisted that it had been three weeks and there was no way it was going to influence his racing, but the vet said that in Pennsylvania the rules were very strict, the medication was illegal for racing, and he was told to pull the horse from the race. I couldn't argue it. So my horse was scratched in a race that I could have easily won $10,000. I was sick.

So I had to pack him up, take him back to Maryland and take the loss. I was fined $250.00, I had to go back to Pennsylvania, go before the steward, pay the fine and even though I brought the vet with me who stated that the drug was legal in Maryland and I had done nothing wrong, I didn't have a leg to stand on. So I paid the fine and left. Lesson learned. That was the first and only time I had a horse test positive. And it was innocent on my part. Many more do it on purpose and hope to slip through. Sometimes they do and other times they do not. I can only say that it wasn't anything I would ever do knowingly.

Author's note: I asked Ray to describe a typical day in a driver's life:

You get up around 6:00 a.m. and get to the barn around 7:00. The vet is usually there by then and goes down each stall to check horses, give injections or meds if needed and make sure the horses are sound. Temperatures have to be taken on each horse and the vet completes paperwork on the horses describing what if anything he did to each horse. There is a clipboard outside of each stall that the vet enters this information on. From there you start to jog and train. You don't do it yourself. You have second trainers to help. They will have everything all prepped and ready to go. The grooms have already fed the horses and laid out the equipment.

In Chicago we had 36 horses in our stable. We had three trainers, which means that every day those three trainers had to drive 36 horses. Any of the horses that were racing that day or had raced the day before did not get worked. But the rest were taken out onto the track and did a total of three trips around.

The first time around a trainer goes easy on the horse. This round just loosens the horse up. Then he is taken back to the stall, blankets are put on him, let him sweat out a bit and then back to the track. In this next heat the trainer pushes the horse a little faster but not full out yet. The horse is toweled down again and then in last heat the trainer gets the horse to that last quarter and lets him open up. This heat is for speed. You never use him for the full mile though. This is just for training.

Then of course, the horse is jogged every day. Normally most people jog their horses between 3-5 miles. My wife and I had different ideas when it came to the training our horses received. We jogged them up to ten miles a day and then water trained! We used an Australian method. Most Americans didn't like that way, saying it was crazy and not necessary, but we swore by it. I learned that when the Australians came over for the World Cup one year.

One team came to stay at Hervé Filion's farm. I happened to be his blacksmith at the time and was living there with my wife and daughter. It was probably around 1982. Anyway, I became real good friends with them and they taught me so much. It was their belief that the American horses they had competed against didn't have the stamina their horses had.

"Your horses jog for three miles a day and then you bring them back in the stalls," one fellow told me. "Then you put him in a race and expect him to go full out for the mile. That horse isn't in condition for that."

"Well, what more would you have me do?" I questioned.

"We take a bar and put it behind a tractor and pull as many as ten horses behind that tractor and while someone drives. The horses can gallop, jog, or do whatever they want for ten miles or so. Then after that is done, we put them in the river to swim. We attach ropes to each side, put the horse out in the middle of the river, and a man stands on each side and holds on, and that horse has to swim! Believe me, these horses get conditioned."

Now we had a big swimming pool at the farm. So we decided to give it a try. We would put the horses in and swim them in a circle while we walked around. Well, when the Australians saw what we were doing they had more advice.

"Why do it that way?" one asked. "You are taking them in one direction and you are only using one half of the horse's muscles."

"Yeah, you're right. But how would I use all of his muscles?" I was puzzled.

"What we do we just tie him off and let him swim."

"Well, if we did that he would just swim to the side and try to get out of the pool!"

Then I started to think. I was sure I could come up with something.

Well, from there I developed a hitch that attached to the horse's tail and wouldn't pull the hair out or hurt the horse. First I drilled into the concrete floor of the ramp that the horses used to enter the pool and I screwed in a large O-ring. I then attached an 8 ft. rope to this hitch I had made, which was now attached to the horse's tail, and I put a hook on the end of shorter lead line with a clamp. Then I would hold the 8 ft. rope to lead the horse, and when he entered the water down the ramp into the pool, and went past the ring on the floor, I would reach down and clip the hook that was attached to the hitch into the ring.

Now the horse has to swim in the middle of the pool and not just around in a circle. He is in a stationary position because his tail is being held firm. To stay afloat he has to use both front legs to swim and at the same time he is setting his spine. The pressure on his tail and him pulling forward is helping to keep his spine straight. Going in a circle all the time keeps that spine curved. That can't be good! Think about it. It makes perfect sense. Instead of using one front leg to pull himself around in a circle, he is using all legs together to swim straight. Everything is aligned and he is working every muscle.

We would start the horses out slow. Maybe two minutes to begin with and then five and then seven and then ten until we worked them up to forty-five minutes!

Well, later when other trainers saw what I was doing, they thought I was plumb crazy!

"What the hell are you doing?" one said.

"I'm swimming the horse to use all of his muscles," I replied. None of the trainers agreed, but I had the results to show for it. I had winning horses that were in top condition and could perform well on the track. If you reached up and tapped any of my horses, they went forward. They had great lungs and could withstand the runs easily. That was all I needed to know to be a believer.

Today many training facilities still use the pool, but now they are long and narrow (about 5 ft. wide) to facilitate the horse's swim, and use the hitch and clip that I developed. They have a ramp to enter and an exit ramp at the other end for the horse to get out of the pool. The horses walk in, exercise and can walk out of the pool when they are finished.

Author's note: Hervé Filion played an important role in Ray Smith's career. According to the Canadian Horse Racing Hall of Fame, by the time Hervé Filion was inducted into Canada's Horse Racing Hall of Fame at the age of 36, the legendary horseman from Angers, Quebec, had already compiled nearly six thousand driving wins. More than thirty years later that number had ballooned to just over fifteen thousand, making Filion the winningest driver in the history of North American harness racing. A total that was also nearly 3,000 more wins than his nearest competitor. Filion, who continued to drive approaching his 70th birthday, has reined the winners of over $88 million. In 2007 he was active at Pocono Downs, Pa.

Known for both his unworldly gift in a race bike and his unmatched work ethic, Filion won 16 seasonal dash titles in his career, recordings even in a row from 1968 through 1974. In 1968 Filion won a then-record 637 races, a mark that stood until 1986 when fellow Hall of Famer and Quebec native Mike Lachance bettered the mark. Two years later

Filion regained his crown, winning a then-record 798 races in the first of three straight dash crowns. A year later, he surpassed his own record with 814 wins. Though three others have broken that record, it stands as Filion's personal best. It's been an impressive career for the determined man with nine siblings raised on the family farm in Quebec. "We were poor when I was a kid. Three boys to a bed and two horses to a stall." As a boy Hervé gave up hockey in favor of horses, constantly spending what time he could with them. "I guess I was about 11 when I started thinking about being a driver."

Hervé was hoisted into a sulky race for the first time when he was 13 at Rigaud, Quebec. He won the race with Guy Grattan, which incidentally paid a handsome win. His determination to succeed soon had Hervé studying the performances of other drivers. He chose future Hall of Fame inductee Keith Waples as one to pattern himself after. Waples' unique style of being able to shift the bike around in tight quarters was a tactic that Filion adopted and refined to what many observers call the Hervé Hop. "I can move a sulky maybe two feet to the right or to the left," Filion said. Hervé and his brothers (all of whom became licensed drivers) branched out from Angers to tracks in Quebec and Ontario before moving to the United States.

In his heyday, Filion often drove six or seven races at a matinee in New Jersey, and then flew by helicopter to New York for six or seven drives at either Roosevelt or Yonkers. Many times after driving in an early race or two at the New York tracks he would sneak behind the tote board and hop a helicopter for a short ride to the airport, where he would board a private jet flight for a flight to Toronto and a drive in a stakes feature at Greenwood Raceway. The hustle paid off for Filion. He would make numerous appearances at small tracks instead of resting in comfort at home. One cold winter's day at Orangeville Raceway he was thrown from the sulky as though shot from a cannon. He flew high and landed on his shoulder, but rolled to his feet, clear of oncoming horses. The incident didn't bother him a bit and he was back in the sulky for the next race. There were thoughts that an outstanding career might have ended that afternoon for a big-name driver on a track known to few people outside Ontario. He told one U.S. writer, "Look, I'm here because I owe the sport. It has been good to me. I should give something back." Filion was fond of saying, "If I wasn't doing this, I'd be carrying a lunch pail to work every day."

Among the quantity of horses was a fair share of quality performers. He upset the great Albatross with Nansemond in The Little Brown Jug; he won the Dexter Cup with Marlu Pride and the Realization Pace with Adios Waverly, Keystone Pebble and Otaro Hanover. In 1986, Filion drove Quebec's great trotting mare Grades Singing. In 1970 he gained more notoriety when he won five races on one card at Brandywine, Del., each in less than two minutes. At Windsor Raceway he also won seven races on a single program. That year, 1971, he was named the winner of the

Lou Marsh trophy as Canada's Professional Athlete of the Year. Filion also received the Medal of Honour from Prime Minister Pierre Trudeau; he won a Hickok Professional Athlete Award; he earned several United States Trotting Association awards; he was the Horseman of the Year, as voted by the Canadian Trotting Association and has been Harness Tracks of America Driver Of The year. In 1975, he became the youngest person ever inducted into the U.S. Harness Racing Hall of Fame. As U.S. Hall of Fame great Billy Haughton once said, "There are a lot of good harness drivers, a few great ones... and then there is Filion."

Ray continued with his story:

Okay, now back to a typical day. After the horses are trained and jogged, which takes a couple of hours, the grooms bathe the horses, and you better grab a bit to eat. Because once the races begin you can't leave the area. Say you have a horse in the third race and then not again until the 10th race, you still can't leave the area. So eating whenever you can becomes important. When we were in Chicago, we lived an hour away, so it wasn't practical to go home before the races began. But In Pompano we lived close so we would head back to the house to eat and then be back where we needed to be for race time.

Once we were back at the track the pre-race testing would begin. Each horse was tested for drugs, tack is checked and horses are readied. Now the testing doesn't only refer to the horses. The drivers are checked too. You may not drink or do drugs while you are a driver. If you do you WILL get caught. There are regulations that are in place to protect not only the driver, but also the horses and spectators. Drinking and drugs have no place on a track.

Breathalyzer tests are always given to the drivers. Drug testing is a bit different. You never know when they will ask you to test or to give a urine sample. Anytime you are in paddock, officials can tap you on the shoulder and ask you to follow them. And you WILL do as they say. Believe me they take this very seriously. They may test you today, and next week or maybe a month from now. You never know. So you have to be prepared and clean.

Once the racing is over for the night, you have to make sure horses are cooled down, checked for injuries and that each one is taken care of before they are bedded down for the night. Usually your second trainer will handle most things for you, but if you have an injured horse, you are probably there for the night. We never leave a sick horse until we know things are okay. That is our responsibility.

Basically that is how it is seven days a week, 12 months a year. Drivers don't get much time off, unless they want it. But if you start refusing races, you won't get asked again. You have to be available when the owners need you. Unless you are totally devoted to the business and it's in your blood, then you don't belong there.

Author's note: While we talked, Ray's grandson, Rejean Sylvain Savard entered the room. Jean (pronounced Gene), as he is called, sat down with us for a few minutes. His father, Jean Marc Savard, had been Hervé Filion's trainer for ten years. People would say that while Hervé had "golden hands" when it came to horses, Jean had "silver hands". This man was probably the best trainer Ray had ever seen. And Ray's grandson showed promise of following in his father's footsteps. When Ray's grandson Jean was only about 6 years old, he raced his pony for fun against another pony his father drove and beat him! He was so little that his feet did not reach the stirrups so Ray put his feet up on the shaft and the young boy went on to out-fox his father.

Rejean's mother Debra had been a groom for Hervé Filion and the family had high hopes that young Jean would grow up to be a driver, but unfortunately he had allergies and being in the barns just didn't agree with his system, so their hopes were dashed. However today Jean has a good knowledge of harness racing, having been around it for most of his life.

I asked Jean to explain how the drivers today set times so much faster than they did back when Ray was driving:

"I believe that breeding plays an important part. The horses today are better conditioned and they are bred better. When you think about it, a driver is only as good as his horse. The higher the breeding and quality of a horse, the more wins you are going to rack up.

"Equipment also comes into play. The bikes today are so much better. The seats are back farther so you can get more lift on the front, which contributes to speed. The harness rigging is better too."

Author's note: There are several types of breeding but in harness racing, outcrossing is often used. Outcrossing produces horses that do not have common ancestors within five generations. They join the finest sire and dam of two existing bloodlines and it produces sound horses with the best of both. Outcrossing produces many more pacers than trotters.

Most trotters are line bred, which means breeding to just the male line of a pedigree or breeding a sire line to a broodmare sire line.

In-breeding is the mating of dam to son, or sire bred to daughter, the two most commonly practiced. There may be several other close variations of in-breeding, brother and sister, half-brother and sister, dam to grandson, sire to granddaughter. In-breeding has been found to be most successful where there has been a previous successful outcross.

On another subject, I asked Ray what a driver gives up when he chooses racing for his life:

You have to love this business and be totally committed to it to make it work. But you sacrifice a lot. You give up a normal family life, your social life is pretty much non-existent and your only friends are the other drivers. You don't have the freedom to take days off when you feel like it. Vacations are not possible because as I mentioned earlier, if you start turning down races, owners will not offer them to you later and you lose your income. You are constantly moving and going here and there. It really isn't a life that mixes well with marriage and families for most drivers. I decided early on that Marilyn would go with me whenever I traveled. Lucky for me she was just as much into the racing and it worked for us. It was a way of life for us.

You have to want it really bad to live this kind of life. It's no different from bull riding, baseball and football players and the like. When you are in sports, you are on the road, spend most of your time in hotels and believe me that can get tiresome after a while. If you are willing to make the sacrifices then it's a personal choice. I don't know that I would recommend harness driving to a young person as a career unless it is something they plan on putting the time and effort into. It takes perseverance and drive to succeed in this business. It is not an easy life. It can be very lonely.

Take the everyday things that most people take for granted, like food or clothing shopping. Drivers don't have time for that. You don't have time to go and shop around for cars or daily trips to the convenience store. Your day is tied up at the track from the time you wake up until the time you go to sleep at night. That track is the only thing on your mind. Some times Marilyn and I would be eating breakfast at an all night restaurant at 2:00 a.m. because that was the only time we could get away. It is far from what most people consider a normal life.

Marilyn and I had a room at the track and I put a bed in there and a small heater and Marilyn and I would catch a little sleep there whenever we could. This life consumes you.

Beyond that there are too many ways NOT to make money. I mean your horse can be the best in the race and somebody else can make a stupid mistake on the track and you get knocked out and go home that night with no money. You just have to accept it. But in the meantime, the grooms still want to be paid, the feed man wants to be paid, the shoer wants to be paid, the vet wants to be paid, the shipper wants to be paid. So if you don't make any money in a race, you still have to pay your people and you don't eat for a day. That is the financial risk you take when you are a driver. But when you are totally devoted to the business, you just keep going. You look to the next race and you keep on plugging! There are ups and downs in the race world. You find that out very quickly.

Just about the only way to continuously have money coming in is to have your own stable of horses. If you have to rely solely on owners, you may not get steady work, but you know you can always depend on your own stable. That way you always have a horse to enter and race. Not everyone can do that but that does ensure that you will have work. I know when we first got into the business Marilyn and I had to have jobs to supplement our income until the point where we had horses of our own to drive. We started with about four horses. That was all we could afford, but slowly we built it up. Being successful in this business takes careful planning.

Another consideration is the problem with medical insurance. Who is going to insure someone that takes their life into their own hands every day racing? No one I know except maybe for Lloyd's of London. If something happens to you on the track or you are killed, your wife and kids get nothing. The track does carry some insurance for hospitalization only. But regular insurance for illness or things like that doesn't exist for the drivers. And there is no such thing as retirement money. That is up to you to plan for. The only exception that I know of is in New Jersey. The Meadowlands Race Track is owned by the state of New Jersey. They take out a certain percentage of the purse money and put it into a fund for each driver. The more you drive, the more your fund builds up. It can be used later as a retirement fund. But at other tracks you are on your own.

So before someone makes the choice to become a harness driver, many considerations have to be explored. This is not the life for everyone.

Author's Note: I asked Ray if there were many black drivers in harness racing and if prejudice played a role in the industry.

Unfortunately, prejudice did exist back when I was racing, and may still exist. I never thought much about it back then because I had a good friend named Charlie who was black. He was invited to our home many times and was like family. While it was normal for us, my neighbors didn't like it too much. For them to see Charlie taking my wife in the truck with him or doing work with us really irked them. I heard a lot of negative remarks, but Charlie and his wife were great people and were very good to us, so I ignored the neighbors. I didn't care whether they liked us or not. It was none of their business.

As for racing, I took a black fellow up to Chicago with me to drive one of my horses one time and they wouldn't let him drive. We drove all night to get there! Well, before the race the officials came up to me and said, “You know, we don’t allow blacks to drive here.”

“Well, I may as well pack my horses up right now and go home. Because I got his name down to drive one of my horses and there is no way I am going to take him off. This man came here to drive and he is going to drive or I am not going to race,” I said, matter of factly. I knew that everyone wanted to see my horse’s race. That’s why they came to the track. “So you go back and talk to your people and let me know. This driver has a license from the USTPA and he has traveled all over the country for me and I am not about to tell him he can’t drive because he is black.”

Well, they came back a while later and said he could race in that one race but no more. That was around 1965. Now the best black driver in the world that I know of was Lou Williams. He was a good friend of mine. In fact such a good friend, that after I was hurt one time, he drove up from New York in his chauffeur driven Mercedes, got out, drove my horses and wouldn’t take a penny for doing it!

The next winter when he came down to Pompano, they would not issue him a license and everyone knew it was because of his color. I told him to get the best lawyer he could. Well he did just that and walked into the track office with a tape recorder along with his lawyer who also had a tape recorder, and he stated that he was only going to ask them one time for a license and if he was not issued that license he would proceed to sue. Believe me, they gave him a license. Prior to that I had put him down to drive on of my horses and they came to me and said he couldn't drive because they were denying him a license. And it was clear it was because he was black.

We used to call him "Sweet Lou". In one night he made $250,000 racing. He was one of the greatest racers I had ever known. Lou had 5 of the top 10 horses at the Meadowlands in his stable. But I guess drugs took over later and he lost everything. He had a cocaine habit. His problem had always been money. He just didn't know how to manage it. Once it became known and they took away his driving license, they also took away his training license and he couldn't make any money, so he had to get rid of his stable and began working on the track doing odd jobs. He came to me one night and had nothing. He was dead broke. I gave him $20. I felt real bad for him. Two weeks later, while driving a tractor on the track, it turned over and killed him.

There may have been other good black drivers but I didn't know of any.

Chapter 6

Author's Note: You can't write a book about harness racing without the mention of Hambletonian. Just about all American harness horses can trace every line of their pedigree directly back to Hambletonian. This American race and stud horse profoundly influenced the sport of harness racing. The stallion was born in Sugar Loaf, New York on May 5, 1849.

Hambletonian was a great-grandson of the imported English thoroughbred Messenger. Sired by Abdallah and foaled by a horse called the Charles Kent Mare, Hambletonian and his dam were owned by Jonas Seeley. Seeley's hired hand, William Rysdyk, cared for them. Rysdyk became so attached to the pair and was so convinced that the foal would someday be great that he asked to purchase them.

Seeley finally agreed, and for $125 William Rysdyk took his prize possessions home.

Hambletonian 10, as he was registered, made his first public appearance at the age of six months at the nearby Orange County Fair in Goshen. He caused quite a sensation and horsemen started referring to him as "Rysdyk's Abdallah colt." This colt began his stud career at age two when Rysdyk allowed him to cover four mares. Meanwhile another son of Abdallah, Abdallah Chief, owned by Seeley C. Roe, was looming as a competitor for the local stallion honors. Roe had nothing but contempt for Hambletonian, and claimed he'd never be a trotter, only a show horse. This issue was settled in 1852 at Long Island's Union Course. Hambletonian and Abdallah Chief were hitched to skeleton wagons with their owners driving. Three minutes and three seconds after the start, Hambletonian crossed the finish line ahead of his rival. Roe still wasn't satisfied and insisted on another race. A time trial was held. Abdallah Chief went the mile in 2:55 1/2. Then Roe watched Hambletonian, in what would be the only time trial of his career, trot the mile in 2:48 1/2. Rysdyk then placed Hambletonian at stud in Chester and bred him to local mares for a fee upwards of $500. The horse's reputation quickly grew as a sire of speed, and Rysdyk made a modest fortune from the horse's services. In his years at stud, 1,331 foals were sired. From four of Hambletonian's sons (George Wilkes, Dictator, Happy Medium, and Electioneer), the lineage of virtually all American standardbred race horses can be traced.

At age 27 on March 27, 1876, Hambletonian died. Both he and his owner, who died in 1870, were buried in Chester, N.Y. Seventeen years after Hambletonian's death a granite monument, the gift of many people who had fond memories of the horse, was placed over his grave on Hambletonian Avenue.

In honor of the "Father of the American Trotter", the Hambletonian Stakes, a United States harness racing event is held annually for three-year-old trotting standardbreds. It is the most coveted North American race for trotters; among races for pacers, only the Little Brown Jug is as prestigious. The Hambletonian is the first, and most prestigious, event in the United States Trotting Triple Crown races.

Chapter 7

When asked what the harness racing world meant to him, Ray has very clear thoughts. He was quick to answer and summed it all up for me during our last interview:

You know people used to say to me, "Why would you ever give up a normal life, owning your home and business, or being for instance a union electrician?" I would just laugh at that statement. For Marilyn and I, it just wasn't what we liked doing or wanted to do with our lives. Ordinary life wasn't fun. If we didn't do anything else, we had fun. We got to travel places we never would have gone to and we got to meet people we never would have met. Do you know how beautiful it is in New England in the summertime? Or in western Australia? Or California? These were experiences that we never could have dreamed having if I had stayed home and led an "ordinary" life being a business owner or an electrician. Not that there is anything wrong with that, don't get me wrong. It just wasn't the life we wanted. But then again, racing isn't for everyone either. It was just a choice we made.

I guess that I just didn't want to be like everybody else. I didn't really care whether people thought I was a good driver or not, or the best trainer in the world. That didn't mean anything to me. What I cared about was the horses, the racing and winning! And I wasn't the kind of horse owner that had to drive my own horses all the time. I mean if I knew there was another driver who could take my horse to the winner circle, then I put that drivers name down. I wasn't stupid! I didn't have an ego problem. I was out to win.

And we did very well. We didn't become millionaires and didn't make near the money I would have if I had stayed in a business, but at the same time we had everything we wanted, the best food, nice quarters to live in, and most important we had each other. We were able to be together every day. That in itself was priceless to me. I know a lot of drivers who because of the nature of the race business were away from home for months at a time. And most marriages don't survive that. It can be a lonely life without family.

In the beginning it was hard, I don't deny that. When we first got into the ponies I was working full time running the business, and racing at the same time. But with the ponies we did that together on the weekends. When we began with the big horses there were times when the kids were small that Marilyn couldn't go with me. But once they got older, I made sure Marilyn was with me all the time. And she shared my love for racing which made all the difference. It was something that we loved together. And we gave it our all.

And when I think back to all of the interesting people we met along the way, it just astounds me. There are a lot of wealthy people in the racing industry. But we all had horses in common; and people were so good to us. I talked to everybody, and maybe that's why I knew so many people. Nobody was a stranger to me. And that helped me in the business.

I have said this before, but if you want to learn things, you have to speak up. I never had any problem asking questions, no matter how stupid they may have seemed to the person I was asking. I wanted to know how they did things and when they talked I listened. I was real good at listening and retaining that information. And at the track you have to be knowledgeable. If you are not, then you may as well hang it up.

What it all boils down to is that if I had chosen another way of life, I know in my heart I would not have been happy. But let's go back to what you asked me much earlier. You asked me how I could have thrown away my trophies. And here is my answer. If that's all that racing meant to me, the trophies, the glory, the money, then that would be my focus. I wouldn't be able to see beyond all of that material stuff. If I let that control my life I wouldn't have time to do the other things I want to do before I die! And that is the truth.

If you live for yesterday, how are you going to prepare for tomorrow? There are a lot of things I have done that I regret. Would I change them? Probably, but at least they were my decisions and I learned from them. I mean would I have built that huge barn if I had known someone was going to burn it down and leave me with nothing? No, but I couldn't have foreseen that happening. And the time I removed my body cast so I could drive in a race? Of course, I wouldn't have done that if I thought I couldn't drive. And I knew that horse better than anyone else. I would never put other drivers in harm's way. But I think back now, and that was probably a pretty dumb thing that I did. But when you're hurt and have no money coming in, you make decisions that you feel are best for you at the time.

We have had such a different kind of life. We enjoyed every minute of it. Lynne, you entitled this book, "The Drive To Glory". To most people that title would mean making it to the winner's circle. It would encompass only the race. To me it has a much deeper meaning. My "Glory" was that I lived my life doing what I loved best. My accomplishments were mine and mine alone. I chose my path and was able to live a dream. I had the best wife, the best kids, the best friends, the best horses, and have no regrets at all. How many people can say that? Not many I would assume. So for me the "Drive to Glory" was the road that led me to today, all the up-hills and the down-hills. It has been a roller coaster way of life and Marilyn and I wouldn't change a minute of it!

Illustration of a harness with full collar

Harness Terms

- A collar to allow the horse to push against the harness with its shoulders and chest. Two main alternative arrangements (with some intermediate types):

- A horse collar (or *full collar*). A padded loop fitting closely around the horse's neck, pointed at the top to fit the crest of the neck. Used for heavier pulling, especially when used without a swingletree or whippletree.
- A breastcollar. A padded strap running around the chest from side to side. Used for light work, or for somewhat heavier work it is used together with a swingletree or whippletree to allow each shoulder to pull evenly on each step without rubbing.

- Hames (if a full collar is used). Two metal or wooden strips which take the full force of the pull, padded by the collar.
- Breeching (pronounced "britching"). A strap around the horse's haunches allowing it to set back and slow a vehicle, usually hooked to the shafts or pole of the vehicle. Used for a single horse, a pair, or in a larger team, only for the *wheelers* (the animal or pair closest to the vehicle). The leaders in a team do not have breeching, as they are in front of the shafts or pole and so cannot slow the vehicle. Breeching may

also be omitted in fine harness, or when the cart is very light or has efficient brakes on the wheels.

- Traces or tugs. The straps or chains which take the pull from the breastcollar or hames to the load.
- Saddle. A small supportive piece of the harness that lies on the horse's back (not the same as a riding saddle).
- Girth. A strap that goes firmly around the girth of the horse to attach the harness saddle.
- Belly-band. A strap that goes more loosely under the belly of the horse, outside the girth. Prevents the shafts rising up, especially on a two-wheeled vehicle (where weight on the rear of the cart may tip the front up).
- Back band. A strap going through the harness saddle to join the belly band either side. Takes the weight of the shafts or pole. In cart harness it is replaced by a chain running in a groove in the harness saddle, hooked to the shafts either side.
    - Sliding back band. In a two-wheeled vehicle the shafts are fixed to the vehicle to hold it level. On a side-slope, one shaft will be higher than the other, and in this case the back band is normally

allowed to slide sideways through the harness saddle, so the horse can walk upright without strain on the harness.

- Fixed back-band. In a four-wheeled vehicle the shafts or pole must be allowed to hinge up and down, to allow the horse and vehicle to pass over hillocks and dips. Often the shafts are independently hinged, and on a side-slope these will each hinge to follow the horse, and a sliding back band is not needed. However, if a sliding back band was used with independent shafts it might allow one shaft to ride up higher than the other, and so for such shafts the back-band is normally fixed to the harness saddle. On other four-wheeled vehicles the two shafts hinge together, and a sliding back band is needed as for two-wheeled vehicles.

- Surcingle. Term used within certain light fine harness designs to describe the combination of a light girth and harness saddle.
- False martingale. A strap passing between the front legs, from the centre of the collar to the belly band, to hold the collar in position. Called "false", because

unlike a true martingale it does not attach to the reins.

- Crupper. A strap attached to the rear of the saddle or surcingle that places a soft padded loop under the base of the tail, to keep the harness from slipping forward.
- Shaft tugs, or just tugs. Loops attached to the back band to hold up the shafts of a vehicle in van or fine harness (not needed in cart harness, which attaches to hooks on the shafts). Two types:
    - For two-wheeled vehicles the tugs are stiff leather loops, fitting fairly loosely around the shafts to allow flexibility as the animal and the vehicle move against each other.
    - For four-wheeled vehicles with independently hinged shafts, the tugs (*Tilbury tugs*) are leather straps buckled tightly around the shafts so they move with the animal.
- Terrets. Metal loops on the saddle and collar to support the reins. The bridles of the rear animals of a large team may also have terrets to take the reins of the animals to the front of them.

- Reins. Long leather straps (occasionally ropes) running from the bit to the driver's hands, used to guide the horses. In teams of several animals these may be joined together so the driver only need hold one pair.
- Bridle. When working in harness, most horses wear a specialized bridle that includes features not seen in bridles used for riding. These usually include *blinders*, also called *blinkers* or *winkers*, behind and to the side of the horse's eyes, to prevent it from being distracted by the cart and other activity behind it. Harness racing horses sometimes have a shadow roll on the noseband of the bridle for the same purpose.
- Bits for harness (most often a Liverpool bit) may be similar to those used for riding, particularly in mouthpiece, usually operating with a curb bit and adjustable leverage to help balance the effect of the reins on different horses in a team.
- Some horses pulling lighter vehicles, particularly at horse shows and other public exhibitions, may have an *overcheck* to assist them in holding a desired head position, and for safety reasons. In some cases a

specially designed running martingale may also be added. A looser overcheck may also be used in a working harness to prevent the horse grazing. The overcheck hooks to a *pedestal* on the harness saddle.

Horse brasses. Brass plaques mounted on leather straps, used for decoration, especially on working harness. Made in a very wide range of designs.

Harness Racing Equipment

<u>Brace Bandages</u> are protective bandages worn by pacers or trotters that adhere tightly to the leg of the horse. Typically they are worn by trotters on the hind legs and help to widen out the animal's gait behind. If worn on the front legs, light cotton quilts are often worn underneath to offer protection.

<u>Buxton</u> (Breast collar) is a combination of straps worn that fits around the neck and between the front legs of the horse. It is used to hold the saddle and girth of the harness in place and keeps it from slipping back along the horse's flanks. The proper name for this piece of equipment is Breast collar, but in harness racing circles it has long been referred to as a "Buxton" because Ohio-based trainer Dick Buxton was the first harness horseman to use this type of breast collar on Standardbreds in the early 1960's. Previously, it had been

used mainly on hunter-jumper horses, and today you can find it used in all horse disciplines.

Check Bit (Overcheck Bit) is the bit that attaches to the overcheck. There are many types of overcheck bits, and all have various functions. Basically this bit helps to balance the horse and gives the driver more control over the horse.

Crupper is part of the harness that attaches to the back of the saddle and runs along the horse's back and under his tail. It is used to help hold the harness in place.

Driving Bit is the main bit in the horse's mouth, which is used for steering/driving. There are many types of driving bits, such as snaffles, D-bits, twisted-wire, double-twisted wire, Frisco-June, side-liners, Dr. Bristol, etc.

Driving Lines are what a driver or trainer uses to steer and control the horse. They are typically made of leather or a synthetic material and connect to the driving bit.

Driving Whip is used by a driver in the race to urge and encourage his horse.

Ear Plugs are small pieces of cotton or rubber placed in a horse's ears in order to reduce the noise a horse can hear. In many cases, high-strung horses are thus easier to control when they do not hear all of the sounds of the other horses during racing or training. Ear Plugs can either be left for the duration of a race, or they can be "pop outs." These "pop outs" have a string attached to them, which runs back to the sulky and is easily grabbed by the driver, who can pull them out when he feels the time is appropriate during the race.

Hand Holds are attached to the driving lines and help to give the driver or trainer leverage in controlling and steering the horse.

Harness is the equipment worn by the horse when racing or training. It includes a saddle, girth, crupper, bridle and driving lines.

Headpole is a straight pole that attaches to a ring on the horse's racing halter and to a strap attaching to the waterhook on the horse's harness at the top of the saddle. The purpose of the headpole is to keep a horse's head straight. There are two types of headpoles: a plain headpole and a burr headpole. The burr headpole is a bit more severe than a plain headpole.

Head Number is the small plastic or metal number that is attached to the top of the horse's bridle so that he can easily be identified during the race.

Hobble Hangers are straps that attach to the harness and hold the hobbles in place on either side of the pacers. Two hangers are near the front legs, one on each side; two hang down on the middle of the horse on each side and one hanger each is found behind the back legs on each side.

Hobbles (also Hopples) are used to help a pacer maintain his gait. They are comprised of two loops, with an adjustable middle portion and they attach to the hobble hangers. The front loop is a bit smaller than the hind loop, and the horse's legs go through each. Trotting Hobbles have gained in popularity in the last decade, with the success of horses such as CR Kay Susie. On trotters, the hobbles fit around the front legs only, and are used to help steady the horse's gait.

<u>Knee Boots</u> are boots worn by both pacers and trotters and are used for protecting the inside of the horse's knees. They come in all shapes and sizes, and can be made of leather, felt or rubber.

<u>Murphy Blind</u> is a small piece of leather that can be attached to a horse's bridle in order to help keep his head straight. It is often used in place of, or in conjunction with, a head pole. In some instances, where a horse might resist a headpole, they will accept a Murphy Blind. This piece of equipment was designed by an old-time horse trainer named Murphy, who thought that if he restricted a horse's vision somewhat, the horse would straighten his head to be able to have unrestricted sight. This idea worked.

<u>Open Bridle</u> is a bridle that does not have blinkers or "blinds" on it, and allows the horse full vision on all sides.

<u>Overcheck</u> is what is used to keep the horse's head balanced. It attaches to the waterhook on the top of the saddle of the harness and is attached to an overcheck bit that goes into the horse's mouth, or to another type of overcheck bit that does not go into a horse's mouth, or to a chinstrap or

chin chain. While many horses can jog and some can train without an overcheck, it is very rare to find a horse that races without one.

Quarter Boots are worn typically by pacers on their front feet to protect their "quarters," the back of their hooves/coronet bands.

Quick Hitch is the coupler on the harness that allows the racing sulky (bike) or training (jog) cart to attach to the horse.

Saddle Pad is the fuzzy, thick pad placed under the saddle of the harness to make the equipment sit more comfortably on the horse's back. These come in various colors.

Saddle Pad Number is the pad worn by the trotter or pacer on their backs during warm-ups and races so that they can be identified.

Shadow Roll is a piece of fleece of various thicknesses that is placed over the nose of the horse and attaches to the bridle. The purpose of the Shadow Roll is to keep the horse from seeing shadows either directly below him or to the sides of him, so that he doesn't jump over them and thus, go off stride (gait). There are several types of Shadow Rolls, such as a brush roll, a turned-up roll, a standard roll, a small roll, and the finger roll - made famous by the great pacing mare Shady Daisy.

Shaft is the part of the racing sulky (bike) that attaches to the arch and runs along either side of the horse's flanks.

Stirrups are found (typically) on the inside of the racing sulky (bike) or training (jog) cart so that the driver or trainer has a place to rest his or her feet.

Sulky is the racing cart or bike. Over the past three decades these racing bikes have evolved and developed into a number of different designs. Originally made only of wood, they now can be comprised of metal, titanium, fiberglass, wood and/or a combination of these.

Tendon Boots are worn on the front legs of the horse for protection, below the knee and above the pasterns.

Tongue Tie is used to keep the horse's tongue from flipping back in his mouth and shutting off his air passage while racing or training, possibly causing him to faint and fall. Tongue Ties are typically made out of nylon or cloth.

<u>Two Ring Martingale</u> (Running Martingale) attaches to the bottom of the harness at the girth and comes up between the horse's front legs. The driving lines go through two small rings at the top of the martingale. The theory is that the lines stay steadied with this (running) martingale and thus keep the horse balanced, even if he or she consistently throws or tosses their head about.

<u>Wheel Disc</u> is a clear or colored plastic disc that covers the racing sulky's (bike's) wheels, and prevents a horse's hoof from going through it.

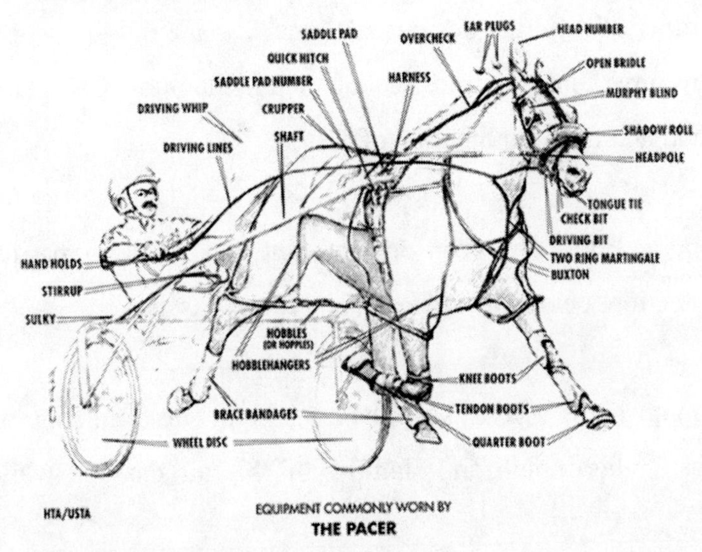

EQUIPMENT COMMONLY WORN BY
THE PACER

Miscellaneous Facts about Harness Racing

Harness racing is a form of horseracing in which the horses race in a specified gait. They also usually pull two-wheeled carts called sulkies, although races to saddle are still occasionally conducted.

In most jurisdictions harness races are restricted to Standardbred horses although cold-blooded horses are raced in Scandinavia. Standardbreds are so called because in the early years of the Standardbred stud book only horses that could trot or pace a mile in a standard time, or whose progeny could do so, were entered into the book.

Standardbreds have proportionally shorter legs than thoroughbreds and longer bodies. They also are of more placid dispositions, as suits horses whose races involve more strategy and more re-acceleration than do thoroughbred races.

Harness races are conducted in two gaits. In continental Europe all harness races are conducted between trotters. A trotter's forelegs move in tandem with the opposite hind legs -- when the right foreleg moves forward so does the left hind leg, and vice versa. In Australia, Canada, New Zealand, the United Kingdom, and the United States races are also held for pacers. Pacers' forelegs move in tandem with the hind legs on the same side.

The founding sire of today's Standardbred horse was Messenger, a gray Thoroughbred brought to America in 1788 and then purchased by Henry Astor, brother of John Jacob Astor. From Messenger, came a great-grandson, Hambletonian 10 (1849-1876), who gained a wide following for his racing prowess. However, it is his breed line that he is most remembered for. From Hambletonian 10's four sons, the lineage of virtually all American Standardbred racehorses can be traced.

Pacing races constitute 80% to 90% of the harness races conducted in North America. The horses are faster and, most important to the bettor, less likely to break stride (a horse which starts to gallop must be slowed down and taken to the outside until it regains stride). One of the reasons pacers are less likely to break stride is that they often wear hopples or hobbles, straps which connect the legs on each of the horse's sides. The belief that hobbles are used to create this gait is a misconception. The pace is a natural gait, and hobbles are merely an accessory to support the pace at top speed, which also ensures safer races.

Most harness races start from behind a motorized starting gate. The horses line up behind a hinged gate mounted on a motor vehicle, which then takes them to the starting line. At the starting line the wings of the gate are folded up and the vehicle accelerates away from the horses. Some European races start without a gate.

The sulky (informally known as a bike) is a light two-wheeled cart equipped with bicycle wheels. The driver carries a long, light whip, which is chiefly used to signal the horse by tapping and to make noise by striking the sulky shaft.

Almost all North American races are at a distance of one mile, and North American harness horses are all assigned a "mark" which is their fastest winning time at that distance. Harness races involve considerable strategy. First of all, drivers may contend for the lead out of the gate. They then try to avoid getting boxed in as the horses form into two lines -- one on the rail and the other outside -- in the second quarter mile. They may decide to go to the front, to race on the front on the outside ("first over", a difficult position), or to race with cover on the outside. On the rail behind the leader is a choice spot, known as the pocket, and a horse in that position is said to have a garden trip. Third on the rail is an undesirable spot, known as the death hole. As the race nears the three-quarter mile mark, the drivers implement their tactics for advancing their positions – going to the lead early, circling the field, moving up an open rail, advancing behind a horse expected to tire, and so on.

Unlike thoroughbreds, harness horses accelerate during the final quarter mile of a race. The finishes of harness races are often spectacular and perhaps more often extremely close. The judges (equivalent to thoroughbred stewards) often have to request prints of win, place, and show photos to determine the order of finish.

Notable harness horses include Dan Patch, a pacer who was the leading sports superstar in the United States in the early twentieth century; Greyhound, a trotter who is arguably the most dominant horse in any era of the sport; Bret Hanover, a pacer; Cardigan Bay, a New Zealand bred pacer who was the first harness horse to win $1 million in North America; Ourasi from France and Mack Lobell of the United States, both trotters, who dominated in the 1980s but who in their one confrontation competed so gamely on the lead that they tired at the end and were overtaken; Cam Fella, a pacer; and Matt's Scooter, a pacer.

The most notable harness tracks in North America are the Meadowlands Racetrack and Freehold Raceway, both in New Jersey, and Woodbine Racetrack and Mohawk Raceway, both in Ontario (harness racing is more popular than thoroughbred racing in Canada). Important Canadian races are the North America Cup (for pacers), the Canadian

Pacing Derby, and the Maple Leaf Trot. Since 1947, the "United States Harness Writers" Association annually votes for the "Harness Horse of the Year." Since inception, a pacer has received the honor 31 times and a trotter 25 times. An outstanding accomplishment for harness horses that has only been accomplished by a few is the Triple Crown of Harness Racing for Pacers and for trotters who make up one in five Standardbreds in racing it is the Triple Crown of Harness Racing for Trotters.

Below are some of the world's great harness pacing horses. Horses underlined and in bold print denote American Triple Crown winner.

Abercrombie
Adios Butler
Albatross
Blissful Hall
Bret Hanover
Cardigan Bay
Dan Patch
Falcon Seelster
Good Time
Hal Dale
Jenna's Beach Boy
Matt's Scooter
Adios
Adios Henry
Billy Direct
Bye Bye Bird
Cam Fella
Countess Adios
Emily's Pride
Forest Skipper
Greyhound
Handle With Care
Mack Lobell
Meadow Skipper

Most Happy Fella
Niatross
Nihilator
On The Road Again
Ourasi
Precious Bunny
Rambling Willie
Ralph Hanover
Romeo Hanover
Rum Customer
Silk Stockings
Sokyola
Star Pointer
Strike Out
Striking Image
Tar Heel
Western Dreamer

The **Triple Crown of Harness Racing for Trotters** consists of the following horse races:

1. Hambletonian
2. Yonkers Trot
3. Kentucky Futurity

Below are some of the great harness trotting horses. Horses underlined in bold print denote Triple Crown winners.

Ayres
Billyjojimbob
Continental Victory
Fresh Yankee
Goldsmith Maid
Green Speed
Greyhound
Hambletonian 10
Lady Suffolk - the "Old Gray Mare"
Lindy's Pride
Lou Dillon

Mack Lobell
Mr. Muscleman
Ourasi
Rodney
Scott Frost
Star's Pride
Victory Song
Windsong's Legacy
Moni Maker
Nevele Pride
Pine Chip
Super Bowl
Speedy Scot
Su Mac Lad
Volomite

Afterthoughts

Harness Racing has been and still is a sport that draws in famous people like celebrities and athletes. George Forman, for instance, has owned more than twenty horses since 1991 and has served as a trophy presenter at the Hambletonian. The list of owners and trainers include Philly pitcher and three-time All Star Dan Plesac and Curt Schilling of the Boston Red Sox.

Other recognizable names are Michael Landon, James Cagney, former New York Jets wide receiver Wayne Chrebet, NHL superstars Wayne Gretzky, Bobby Hull, Darren McCarty and Kris Draper. NBA stars Wilt Chamberlain, Sam Bowie and even NASCAR legend Dale Earnhardt, Sr. also owned some harness racehorses.

Owners and trainers play an important role in the harness business, but it is the drivers who are the real stars.

They possess not only courage, but have to make quick and precise decisions that develop into wins and losses. The trainers turn out the horses but the drivers are the ones who sit behind those horses and transfer that training into big money.

In the time I have known Ray Smith, we have spent a lot of time just talking. Most of our conversations revolved around driving horses and the making of this book. However, the more he spoke, the more I began to realize the true man he was and is. I knew he was knowledgeable about harness racing, horses, training and driving, but beneath all of that there is a gentle, humble man and that is what impressed me the most. He is not a man that is comfortable taking credit for the things he accomplished or the contributions he made to the racing industry. Instead he possesses a humility and appreciation for the life he had while driving. He considers himself lucky to have had the opportunities he had while racing. He enjoyed meeting the people (many of which became close and dear friends), and he always showed everyone consideration and respect no matter who they were.

Ray was then and is now an honest man, always ready to lend a hand to anyone who needs it. He learned early on that you get what you give. He holds the simple belief that when you treat people right, they will treat you right in return.

You read earlier that he threw away all of the trophies he had won. Ray didn't need to tell people what he had done, or show off his trophies or even talk about things he did. He wasn't out to gain any notoriety for himself. He was happy doing what he was doing and he didn't care what others thought about him.

Ray will be the first one to say that he wasn't the best driver in the business. In fact, he made a point to emphasize the influences other people in the industry had on him to make him the driver and trainer he turned out to be. But he put 100% into everything he did during his career. He learned the business and he learned it well. He was the first one to admit his mistakes and not afraid to accept defeat. He never asked anyone to do anything he wouldn't do himself. And he never relied on anyone else to do things for him. Even if he didn't know how to do something, he would attempt it and tackle it until he mastered it. Whether it was learning how to shoe a horse, trying a new apparatus, or dealing with a problem horse, he was willing to work at it. He learned from the best and tried to pass on what he had learned to others. Nothing pleased him more than to share his knowledge.

This man had a different kind of a philosophy than most trainers and treated his horses with kindness and encouragement. That produced some of the finest horses known to the racing industry and he has the records to prove it.

Ray's career in harness racing ended in a terrible accident that left him paralyzed from the waist down. He endured a seven-year recovery and eventually got feeling back and was able to walk again. When I asked him about it, I could see the pain in his eyes. The accident came right after the death of his dearest friend a few months earlier, which was also a track accident. At that point, I didn't have the heart to ask about either accident. I knew from Ray's expression that even after all of these years, it would be too difficult to recount, so I let it be. The details were not important for me to know. I understood what this man suffered. But whatever happened, it did not leave Ray bitter about racing. Instead he to this day respects the industry and cannot say enough about how it impacted his life in a positive way.

Ray will probably be embarrassed when he reads this and he won't see this until the book is published, but this man has been and is now an inspiration to me and I am sure to many others. It has been my sincere privilege to write this book. Ray and Marilyn Smith have not only educated me on the subject of harness racing, but are and always will be my dear friends and I will treasure that forever.